An attitude of the heart that
is self-giving, not self serving.
~ JMR ~

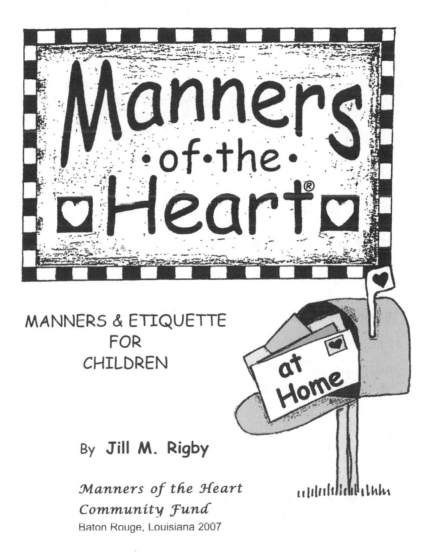

Manners
·of·the·
♡Heart®♡

MANNERS & ETIQUETTE
FOR
CHILDREN

at Home

By **Jill M. Rigby**

Manners of the Heart
Community Fund
Baton Rouge, Louisiana 2007

Copyright © 1999
Manners of the Heart Community Fund

First Edition May 1999
Second printing March 2001
Third printing September 2006
Fourth printing July 2007

Printed in the United States of America

ISBN 1-930236-01-8

Art work by Libby Adams and Jill M. Rigby

Published by
Manners of the Heart Community Fund
Baton Rouge, Louisiana 70808

To our children:

"Tell it to your children,

And let your children tell it
to their children,

And their children
to the
next generation."

-Joel 1:3

TABLE OF CONTENTS

PART THREE
TABLE MANNERS

♥ v ♥

ACKNOWLEDGEMENTS

I am grateful to my mother Evelyn McDonald who taught me the manners of her heart and continues to give her support to every project I undertake.

My twin sons Boyce and Chad have patiently endured countless hours of training in goodheartedness. They are now proving that teenagers can be a joy, not a burden.

I am indebted to Jean Rohloff, my "English professor" and friend, who has used her well-worn pencil to lovingly edit every word I have ever written.

The ladies of my Friday study group have held my hand for many years. We have cried together, laughed together and prayed together. I am thankful for their support and patient love.

My "big sister" Donna Munson has been a steady rock of encouragement. She has listened to hours of my rambling during the planning of the book and offered the invaluable wisdom she gained through raising her daughters.

Ginger Smith has spent the last few weeks deciphering, typing, writing and rewriting *and rewriting* my long hand notes and has patiently helped to complete *Manners of the Heart at Home*.

DEAR TEACHER AT HOME,

Thank you for caring enough to sacrifice your time and energy to share *Manners of the Heart at Home* with your child. Planting the seeds of goodheartedness is one of the noblest tasks a parent can undertake to establish a solid foundation from which your child can grow.

Within these pages, I trust you will find guidance, encouragement and practical suggestions to meet the challenge of teaching your child these important skills. By helping your child gain self-respect through a focus of giving to others, you can instill the tools needed to have humble confidence in all social situations and relationships. If we are helping our children at home to gain self-respect, they will be better students in school.

Manners of the Heart at Home is based on the belief that if respect for others is the foundation of how we treat one another, manners and etiquette will come naturally.

Respectfully Yours,

Jill

Jill M. Rigby

INTRODUCTION

Remember how difficult it was to memorize those unavoidable multiplication and division tables in grade school?

Remember how unimportant learning the names of the generals who led the troops during the Civil War was in sixth grade social studies?

And what about the exam in which you had to match names of the great artists throughout the centuries with their masterpieces in high school art appreciation?

Why do you suppose we were uninterested?

Why do you suppose we thought learning all this information was a waste of time?

At the time, it didn't make sense to memorize all those facts and figures, names and dates. Perhaps it was because we didn't understand the significance of what we were being taught. We didn't understand how this information would benefit our lives in the present. We hadn't yet learned that we weren't being given all this information so that we would simply know a lot or score well on an exam. We were being taught life lessons through math, history, and art that would enable us to one day balance a checkbook, be a leader in the business world, and understand that who we have become as a society today has been shaped by those who have gone before us.

Let's go back and look at an old definition of education. The 1944 edition of *Webster's Unabridged Dictionary* states that education is "the process or manner of training youth for their station in life; the impartation or acquisition of knowledge, skill, and discipline of character." Using this definition, we would define an educator as anyone who imparts "knowledge, skill and discipline" to a child. Our children need to have teachers at school, and they need to have teachers at home.

In the introduction of *Manners of the Heart* (a manners and etiquette curriculum for elementary school children), the point is made that "the role of the teacher, parent or any loving adult is to provide steady, patient guidance in training a child to be respectful." As parents, we need to assist the educational system in training our children. We cannot and should not expect the school to "do it all." We each have a role to play in the educating of our children. These roles often overlap between teacher and parent, especially in the area of training children to be good-hearted. If we are helping our children to gain self-respect at home, they will be better students in school.

If we begin with the following principles that lay the groundwork of good-heartedness, we will have a better understanding of the significance of teaching manners and etiquette:

♥ In defining manners as an attitude of the heart that is self-giving, not self-serving, we can teach our children that manners come from the heart, not from memorizing a set of rules.

♥ Parenting to only build a child's self-esteem can result in a selfish child. Parenting to help a child gain self-respect will result in a selfless child.

♥ Children learn twice as much from what we do than from what we say. Children will imitate our actions and reflect our attitudes, but will often forget our words, unless we model manners of the heart ourselves. The most effective teaching method is by example. Your life must be true to your words.

These principles are at the "heart" of *Manners of the Heart at Home.* By grasping the relevance of these basics, you can teach your children respectfulness, which will lead to an eagerness to learn "all those stupid old rules." (I am quoting many children through the years who have used this as a favorite adjective for rules!)

Gardening is a helpful analogy to illustrate this approach of training children. The first step in gardening is to consult the expert gardeners to determine the right seeds to use. After the selections are made, it's time to cultivate the soil. Extra nutrients will need to be added to enrich the soil and make it well balanced. To help the seeds get off to a good start, special fertilizers will help the plants establish a deep root system that will allow the plants to grow strong and produce an abundance of fruit. During the growth process, we will have to pull weeds, run harmful little creatures out of the garden and continue fertilizing to help the plants reach their full potential. With a lot of tender loving care, sunshine and rain, the garden will begin to produce healthy plants.

Planting the seeds of good-heartedness in your child's heart is the noblest form of gardening. Just as in gardening to raise beautiful sweet crops, we also need to first study so that we can understand the seeds that need to be planted and how to plant them.

We cannot cultivate a successful garden without firsthand knowledge and experience with the seeds of honesty, patience, respectfulness, courtesy, friendship, kindness, and gentleness. As these seeds take root and flourish in our hearts, we can pass them to our children.

♥ x ♥

As you are planting these seeds in your child, extra nutrients will be needed to help them establish a deep root system. Children need a strong foundation on which to build their character. They need support and encouragement from many sources. Teachers, friends, neighbors, relatives, and any patient, loving adult can contribute to a child's growth in good-heartedness. They can add the "fertilizers" that enhance what you have already established. We all can make a difference in children's lives, whether we are part of their immediate family or the extended family of our communities.

Children want to know your history. They want to hear your stories. While teaching the lessons, share yourself with your child. Share your experiences and memories from your childhood. Share your everyday occurrences that illustrate the life lessons.

Model each of the correct ways to accomplish the skills. They will remember much better if they hear you say what to do and then see you do it as well. The more you show your children how applicable these principles are in everyday living, the more readily they will accept them in their own lives.

Manners of the Heart at Home is not about forcing your child to memorize a burdensome set of rules. This approach to training children is about helping your child to gain humble confidence through learning the delicate balance between self-esteem and self-respect. Mastering and maintaining this balance will help to establish a solid foundation, which will carry your child into adolescence with ease.

GROUND WORK

Manners of the Heart at Home is divided into three parts: Everyday Courtesies, Communication Skills, and Table Manners.

We begin with Everyday Courtesies which gives the foundation for all of the lessons. Here we present the principles for being a good-hearted, respectful child.

Next, we present Communication Skills, which helps your child to understand the importance of social graces, such as writing thank you notes and using courteous telephone manners.

To complete the lessons, we teach Table Manners. All the basic mealtime etiquette is presented from using a napkin to eating in a restaurant.

Creative ideas for teaching *Manners of the Heart at Home* and specific instructions are given throughout the book.

PLANTING PLAN

Each lesson is divided into three sections: Objective, Guidance, and Life Lessons, which are described in detail below:

OBJECTIVE: This gives the "teacher at home" the principle goal of the lesson. You can think of this as the seed that will help your child develop goodheartedness.

GUIDANCE: This gives bits of wisdom for teaching and encouraging your child. As you share these bits of wisdom, coupled with your own stories, you will be planting the seeds of goodheartedness.

LIFE LESSON: This gives the "teacher at home" practical applications that reinforce the principles of this approach. As you and your child work together to put these life lessons into practice, you both will reap a harvest of goodheartedness.

MANNERS OF THE HEART
AT HOME
PART 1

EVERYDAY

COURTESIES

WILBUR ♥ PENELOPE ♥ PETER

OBJECTIVE

To teach children an attitude of the heart that is self-giving, not self-serving.

GUIDANCE

"It's not what we gather
that matters,
but what we scatter"
— HELEN WALTON

Talk with your child about manners:

♥ "Manners is an attitude of the heart that is self-giving, not self-serving."

♥ What does that mean to you? It means that it's more rewarding to give to others than to receive.

♥ Goodheartedness is a gift you can give everyday to everyone.

♥ Here are ways to be giving called Everyday Courtesies:

♥ Honesty ♥ Friendship
♥ Patience ♥ Kindness
♥ Respectfulness ♥ Gentleness
♥ Courtesy ♥ The Golden Rule

♥   Being courteous means to be unselfish in all your ways.

♥   Courtesy is being helpful to other people.

♥   To be courteous is to be respectful, cheerful and polite.

♥   Just think, if everyone would be courteous to each other, the world would be a nicer place to live.

LIFE LESSON

♥ Wilbur, Penelope and Peter ♥

Let's make a set of hand puppets! The puppets are made from boxes found in most kitchen cupboards and simple craft materials.   Follow the directions and diagrams to create the characters which will help your child have fun as you teach these lessons on manners.

What you will need:

1 16 oz. brown sugar box
2 16 oz. macaroni & cheese boxes
Construction paper (brown, red, black, white, gray, orange)
Scissors
Glue

Puppet Directions:

A. Close and glue the open end of the box.

B. Mark the center of the box. Cut along marked lines. (front and two sides) Be careful not to cut through the bottom.

C. Fold the box in half, so that the open ends are on the outside.

D. Cover the inside of the box with red construction paper to make the mouth. Cover all other sides with construction paper. (Brown for Penelope & Peter, White for Wilbur)

E. Copy or trace patterns for each puppet. To trace onto construction paper, put the original pattern on top of the paper and draw around the edges of the pattern with a pencil, pressing firmly. Since the construction paper is soft, an impression of the pattern will be left on the paper. Redraw the picture using the impression marks.

C. Following diagrams, glue facial features on to each box.

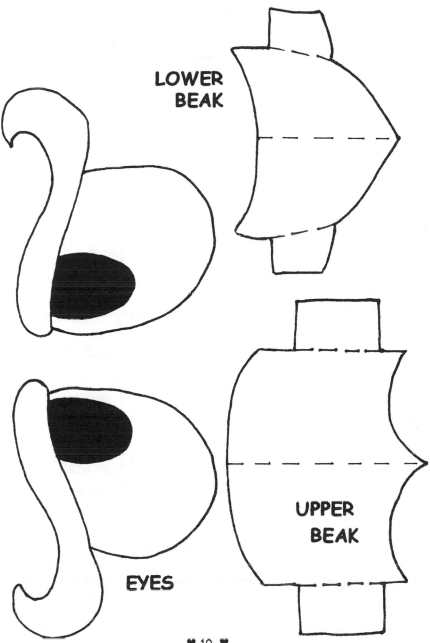

LOWER
BEAK

EYES

UPPER
BEAK

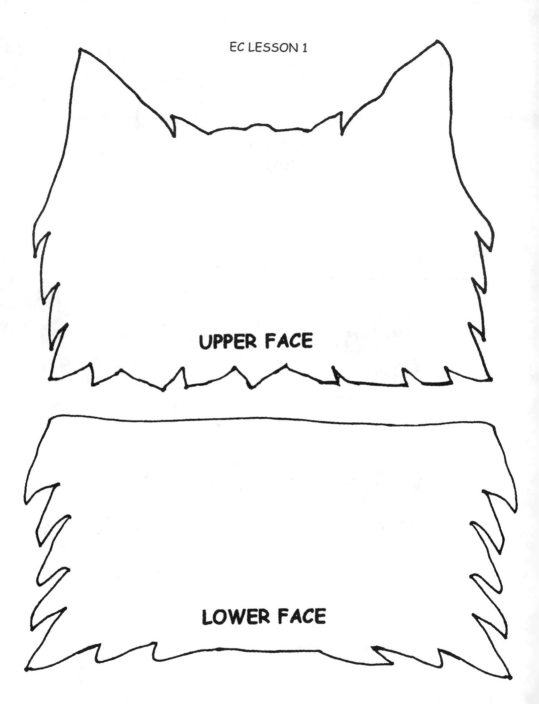

UPPER FACE

LOWER FACE

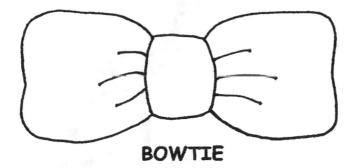

BOWTIE

"WISE OLD WILBUR" PUPPET

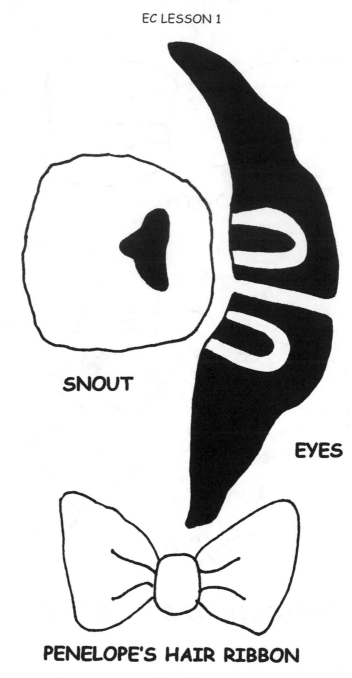

SNOUT

EYES

PENELOPE'S HAIR RIBBON

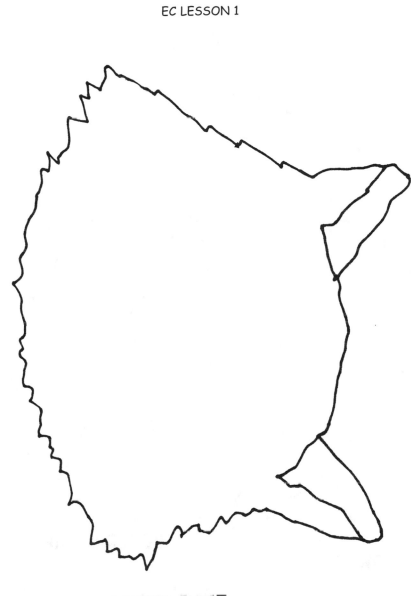

UPPER FACE

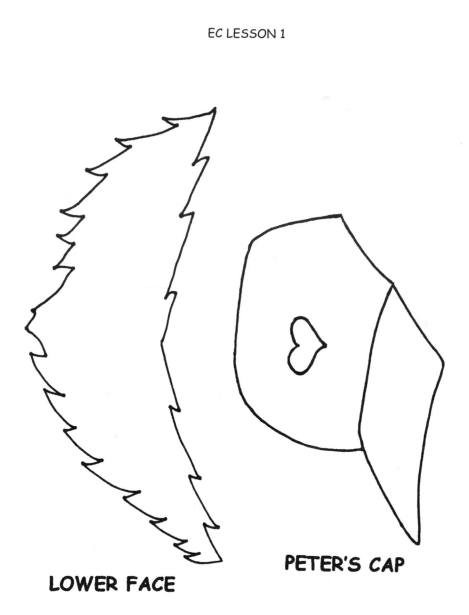

LOWER FACE

PETER'S CAP

PETER PUPPET

PENELOPE PUPPET

SMILE

OBJECTIVE

To teach your child how much a warm smile means to others.

GUIDANCE

"Laugh and the world laughs with you."
We can also say,
"Smile and the world smiles with you."

Share these thoughts with your child:

♥ Do you know that you carry a gift for others with you everywhere you go, all day long, everyday? Do you know what this gift is? A SMILE.

♥ Sometimes all it takes is a smile to turn someone's day around.

♥ Anyone you meet, whether they're young or old or even if they speak a different language, can understand a smile.

♥ A pleasant expression on your face radiates warmth to those around you.

♥ If you were choosing a friend to play with on the playground, wouldn't you choose someone who had a smile and looked happy?

♥ *Webster's Unabridged Dictionary* defines a smile as, "showing pleasure by an upward curving of the mouth and a sparkling of the eyes."

♥ A smile is a frown turned upside down.

LIFE LESSON

♥ Smile Down ♥

Remember as a child when you played "stare down"? You and a friend locked eyes with each other until one of you cracked a smile, laughed, or looked away. The stone-faced player became the "winner."

Play a different version of the game with your child called "smile down." Take turns with one of you being the "smiler" and the other the "frowner." The frowner will try not to return the smiler's grin. Of course, this is impossible! When the frowner smiles, *both* of you win.

Encourage your child to become a "smile giver" by playing this game with those they come in contact with throughout their week. Agree with your child that you will join them in playing "smile down" with others.

You may want to purchase inexpensive smile stickers that you and your child can share with others as you practice this exercise.

You will enjoy sharing with each other the reactions you received from those with whom you've shared your smiles.

RESPECT FOR ADULTS

OBJECTIVE

To teach your child the importance of respect.

GUIDANCE

One of the most important lessons a child can learn is respect.
This is the essential quality of good character.

Share these ideals with your child:

♥ Say "Yes, Sir" and "Yes, Ma'am" when answering your parents, as well as all adults.

♥ Do your chores without grumbling:

  ♥ making your bed   ♥ washing the dishes
  ♥ picking up your toys   ♥ folding laundry

♥ Don't slam doors.

♥ Offer to help Mom or Dad around the house.

  ♥ take out the garbage
  ♥ rake the leaves
  ♥ feed your pet

♥ Come the <u>first</u> time you're called.

♥ Give a hug "just because."

♥ Accept "no" without complaining.

♥ Be cheerful in the mornings.

♥ Say "thank you" often.

♥ Compliment your parents.

 ♥ "Mom, your hair looks great."
 ♥ "Dad, thank you for taking care of us."

♥ Have a good attitude when your teacher corrects you.

 ♥ Respond with "I'm sorry" and "Yes, Sir."
 ♥ Work hard during your class time.
 ♥ Pay attention to your teacher's lessons.

♥ Offer to help with heavy packages.

♥ Talk to adults. Really, they won't bite you. Ask for their advice, especially your grandparents and older relatives.

♥ Call your grandparents often. Write to them if they live in another city.

LIFE LESSON

♥ GoodHearted Box ♥

Enlarge the GoodHearted Box pattern and make a copy for you and your child, along with copies of the heart reminders sheet. (Copy the page on card stock or glue two sheets together to make the boxes stronger.)

Color and cut out your GoodHearted Boxes.

Fold each box on the dotted lines and glue the tabs inside each box to form the sides.

Cut out and fold the heart reminders and place a set in each box. You can make your own reminders for areas of disrespectfulness that you need to address.

Agree that you and your child will draw a reminder each week from your boxes to help you both develop goodheartedness.

For example, if your reminder says "thankful," let your family know how much you appreciate their love. Find one new "thanksgiving" every day and share your discovery with your child.

If your child's reminder says "helpful," suggest that she offer to help with the dishes after supper or help a sibling with a chore. Encourage her to make an extra effort to lend a hand to others throughout the coming week.

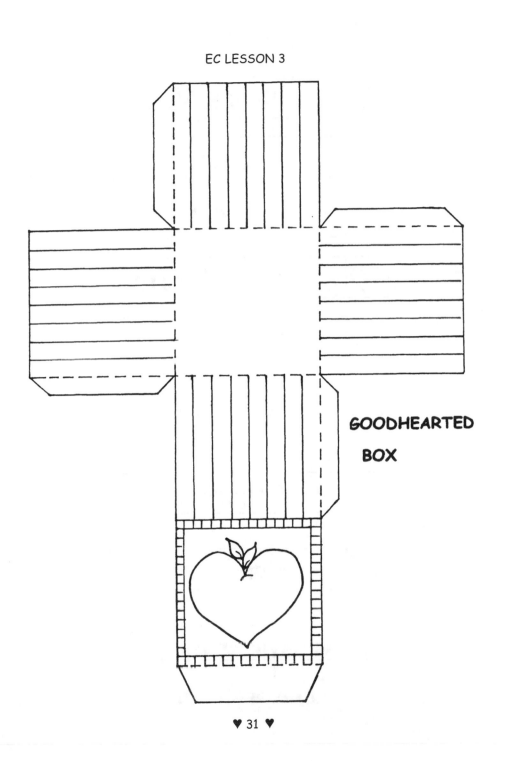

GOODHEARTED

BOX

♡ **Thank You**

♡ **Excuse Me**

♡ **Helpful**

♡ **Considerate**

♡ **Kind**

♡ **Friends**

♡ **Generous**

♡ **Honest**

♡ **Trustworthy**

HEART REMINDERS

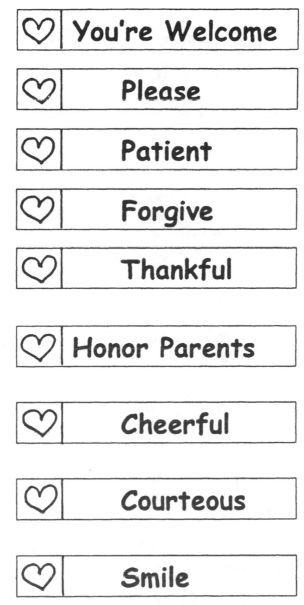

♡ You're Welcome

♡ Please

♡ Patient

♡ Forgive

♡ Thankful

♡ Honor Parents

♡ Cheerful

♡ Courteous

♡ Smile

HEART REMINDERS

BROTHERS & SISTERS

<u>OBJECTIVE</u>

To teach your child at a very young age to live at peace with siblings, so that they can get along with others.

<u>GUIDANCE</u>

> The place to learn
> how to get along with
> others is at home.

Share these thoughts with your child:

Ask your child: "Can brothers and sisters be friends, too?"

It's important to be "friends" with your siblings. Your brothers and sisters will be with you for your lifetime. You can learn a lot about getting along with others when you practice it at home.

There's a lot <u>you</u> can do to live at peace with your siblings:

- ♥ Offer to help with their chores.

- ♥ When they're busy or not feeling well, be understanding.

- ♥ Give compliments often.

♥ Cheer for them at their sporting events.

♥ Encourage them when they're working on special projects.

♥ Stand up for each other.

♥ Don't <u>ever</u> tattle, unless your brother or sister is in danger.

♥ Take turns. When your give your brother or sister a turn first, you'll get a turn in return.

♥ Share the bathroom.

> ♥ Don't stay in the bathroom longer than is necessary.
> ♥ Pick up your wet towels.
> ♥ Wipe the spilled water around the sink.
> ♥ Rinse the toothpaste from the sink after you finish brushing your teeth. Leave it clean for the next person.

♥ Don't spend too much time on the telephone. Remember you're not the only one in the house who likes to use the telephone.

♥ Remember to treat your brothers and sisters like you treat your friends. Treat them like very special guests.

♥ Remember, treat others the way you want to be treated, especially at home. Sometimes we're so comfortable at home, we forget that our siblings are real people. We should always be kindest to our family.

LIFE LESSON

♥ Unexpected Delight ♥

Ask your child: "What's something special that your brother or sister would like?"

Make a list of those suggestions and have your child choose one to put into action.

Here are some additional suggestions:

Suggest that your child do one of their sibling's small chores, to show kindness and thoughtfulness. (make their bed, do their after-dinner chore, etc.)

Make something special for the sibling: a book mark with their name on it, a special picture, a poem about their relationship, a certificate for "THE BEST SISTER IN THE WORLD," a batch of their favorite cookies, etc.

FRIENDS

OBJECTIVE

To teach your child how to be a good friend.

GUIDANCE

"To have a friend, you must be a friend."

Share the following thoughts with your child:

♥   We all need friends. We're not meant to spend our days alone. How do you find friends? You find friends, by first being a friend.

♥   All the qualities that you would want in a friend, you need to have in yourself.

♥   Introduce yourself. Be friendly, cheerful, fun to be around – not a complainer or whiner; not a tease or someone who talks ugly about other people.

♥   Be honest. Learn to keep your friend's secrets. Don't tell others secrets your friend has shared with you.

♥   Share your things with other children without being asked.

♥   Be slow to get angry.

♥   Be quick to say, "I'm sorry."

♥ Ask someone you've just met to sit with you at lunch.

♥ If you're on the playground, ask a new child if they want to play a game with you.

♥ Ask lots of questions of other children when you first meet.

    ♥ Where do you live?
    ♥ What's your favorite sport?
    ♥ Do you have any pets?

♥ Listen more than you talk.

Ask your child: "Will you make a new friend today?"

LIFE LESSON

♥ Friend Fair ♥

Host a Friend Fair for your child and his friends as a fun way to promote friendship. You can plan the fair for an afternoon after school or one morning during a holiday break. If the group is young (Kindergarten through 2nd grade), ask older children to be hosts and hostesses. Encourage your child to include children he hasn't gotten to know yet, in addition to including his closest friends. Remind him to be goodhearted in choosing his guests by treating all of his peers, even the ones who are "different" or "not well liked," the way *he* would want to be treated.

The "Admission Ticket" can be reproduced and given to guests as an invitation.

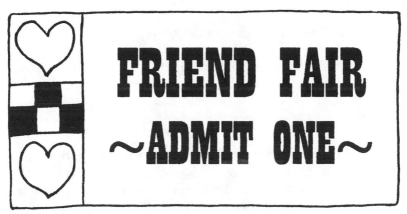

Following are suggestions for three activities:

- ♥ Fish and Tell
- ♥ Colossal Cup Challenge
- ♥ Huff and Puff Boat Race

♥ Fish and Tell ♥

This activity combines a charming, old-fashioned carnival game with a life lesson about making new friends and getting to know old friends better.

What you will need:

Heavy weight string or yarn
Clothespins
Long sticks for making fishin' poles
Large sheet or blanket
Construction paper
Scissors
Tape
Brown paper lunch bags or clear sandwich bags
Candy, tiny trinket, or homemade goodies

Playmate Pond: (See illustration page)

You will use the sheet (or blanket), clothespins, string, construction paper, scissors, tape, and markers.

A. Here are different options for constructing the "pond."

  1. You can hang string across a doorway and attach the sheet to the string (clothesline style) with clothespins. Another option is to drape it over the line. It should be low enough for the child to throw his "hook" over. Make sure you can fit behind it with your "fish favors" and remain unseen

  2. The sheet can also be draped over a sofa, across several chairs, etc.

B. Make a fish favor bag for each child attending from a brown paper lunch bag or a clear sandwich bag. You and your child can decorate the bags a few days before the fair. Fill each bag with candy, trinkets, or homemade goodies. Place behind the playmate pond.

C. Photocopy or trace the fish pattern onto white paper or construction paper. Make two for each child attending the Friend Fair. Separate into two stacks.

D. Print one question from the list below on the back of each fish from one stack. (For younger children who can't yet read these questions, simply print one word asking for a favorite: Ex: Color?, Animal?, etc. Ask the older children to help the younger children read the questions.)

  1. What's your favorite animal and why?

2. How many brothers and sisters do you have?
3. What is your favorite color?
4. What do you like best about school?
5. What's your favorite cartoon and why?
6. What's your favorite holiday and why?
7. What's the funniest movie you ever saw?
8. Tell me the best joke you know.
9. If you could choose your supper tonight, what would it be?
10. If you could go anywhere in the world, where would you go?

E. Let the children write their names on a fish from each stack when they first arrive. Add the fish with the question on the back to a favor bag and adhere the other to the playmate pond. As the children place their fish in a bag, write their name on a sticky note and attach to the outside of the bag.

Fishin' pole:

You will use a stick for each child, string, and clothespins.

A. Demonstrate how to make the pole as each child constructs his or her own.

B. Cut the string the length of the pole plus 12 inches. Tie it securely to one end of the pole.

C. Tie the clothespin to the other end, knotting securely.

Playing the game:

A. Be careful that no one receives their own bag by checking the names on the sticky notes. Remove the sticky note before "releasing" the favor bag to the happy fisherman!

B. Let each child have a turn fishin'.

C. Ask them not to peek in their fish favor bags until everyone has had a turn.

D. When everyone has had a turn, shout out, "FISH AND TELL!"

E. Ask them to "fish out" the paper fish from their bags, find the person who's name is written on it and ask the question on the back.

F. They can enjoy the rest of their "catch" while they get to know each other better.

FISH TAG

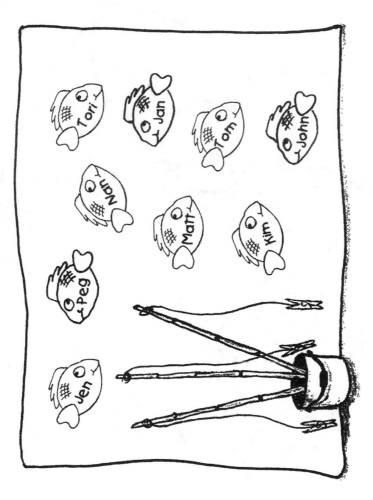

FISH AND TELL

♥ Colossal Cup Challenge ♥

This game is a delight and a challenge to both children and adults, which helps to develop patience as the children wait their turn. Encourage the children to cheer for each other.

What you will need:

Yard stick
5 plastic cups (16 oz. red or blue plastic works well, but fast food cups can also be used.)
Pushpins
Small object to toss, such as ping pong ball, bean bag pennies, etc.

Making the game:

A. Allow your child to decorate each cup with markers or cutouts from magazines. Encourage him to use his imagination and be creative.

B. Place cups at 2", 10", 18", 26", and 34" on the yardstick. (If you are not using a yardstick, place the cups five inches apart.)

C. Insert a pushpin through the bottom center of each cup and push the pin into the yardstick at the proper points.

Playing the game:

A. Place the cup challenge on the floor or ground. Mark a "fault" line 24 inches from end of yardstick for the children to stand behind.

B. Have the children line up behind the line.

C. Each child takes a turn and starts the game by throwing the ball in the cup closest to him. If he makes it in the first cup, he proceeds to the second cup and so on.

D. The turn ends when the child misses.

E. The next child takes a turn. When the rotation comes back around the player picks up from where he stopped his previous turn. (I.e. Second cup, Third cup, etc.)

F. Give a prize to any child that conquers the Colossal Cup Challenge by landing the ball in the fifth cup.

♥ Huff and Puff Boat Race ♥

What you will need:

Pint milk carton
White paper
4 thin sticks or straws
Clay or hot glue
String

Making the boats:

A. Make sure to demonstrate the step by step construction as each child makes his boat.

B. Wash, rinse, and dry as many one pint milk cartons as needed. (Two boats can be made from each carton.)

C. Carefully mark center of carton and cut in half to make two pieces.

D. Glue open end closed. Secure with clothespin while drying.

E. Punch a hole in the center of the boat's back side.

F. Trace sails' patterns. Cut 2 small, 1 large, and 1 flag for each boat. Each child can personalize his sails with markers, crayons or other decorations.

G. Cut slits in sails and flag as marked.

H. Weave stick or straw into slit at bottom of sail and out the slit at top of sail.

I. Secure the sticks or straws with sails to the bottom of the boat with hot glue or clay. The large sail should be placed in the center of the two small sails.

J. Thread the string through the hole at the back of the boat and tie a knot on the outside. Then wrap around the top of each sail several times ending at the flag. The string should be taut. Trim excess. (Refer to illustration of boat.)

The Race:

A. Here are some suggestions for your race "track":

    1. A small children's pool
    2. A large rectangular pan (the water doesn't have to be deep) or tin tub.

B. Two children can race each other at a time or all the children can race at once, depending on how big the container of water is.

C. Each child can propel their boat by blowing through a straw aimed at the sails.

D. If there is only room for one boat in your container, conduct a timed raced in which each child blows his boat across the water. Reward the child that can get his boat across the fastest.

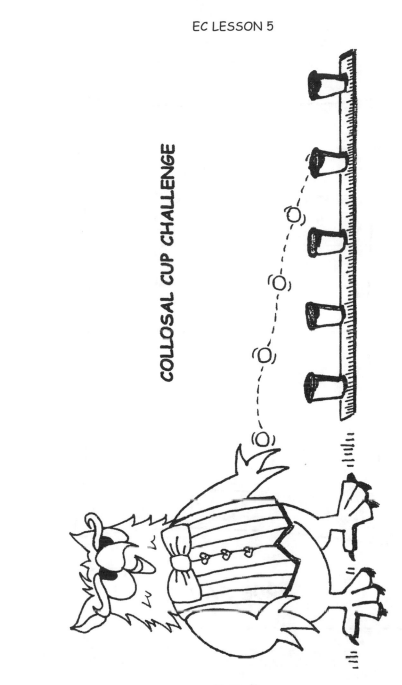

COLLOSAL CUP CHALLENGE

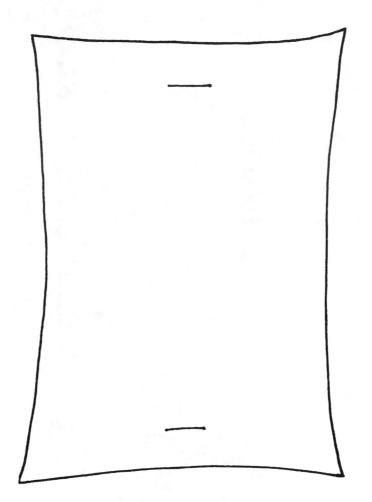

LARGE SAIL

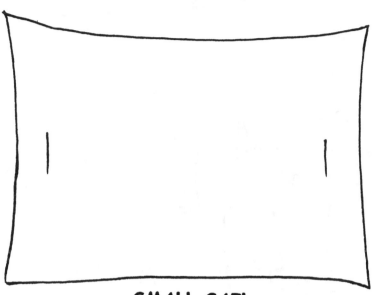

SMALL SAIL

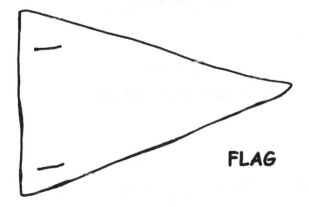

FLAG

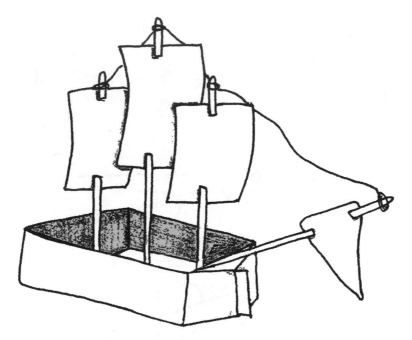

HUFF AND PUFF BOAT

THANK YOU, PLEASE

OBJECTIVE

To teach your child how to be courteous and good-hearted everyday.

GUIDANCE

To be courteous and good-hearted, you must be:

- ♥ Considerate   ♥ Gentle   ♥ Honest
- ♥ Gracious   ♥ Kind   ♥ Forgiving

Share the following thoughts with your child:

♥ Remember, you're learning to think about others ahead of yourself. To have all these good qualities you need to work on forming good habits.

♥ The "magic" words need to be part of your everyday talk.

- ♥ "Thank You"   ♥ "You're welcome"
- ♥ "Please"   ♥ "Excuse me"

♥ Adding "please" to the end of a question turns your question into a pleasant request. "May I borrow your scissors, *please*?"

♥ Whenever someone offers a compliment or does a kindness toward you in any way, respond with "Thank you."

♥ When someone says, "Thank you," your reply should be "You're welcome."

♥ If you have to interrupt someone's conversation with an important message, what should you say? "Excuse me, please."

♥ If you accidentally bump into someone, what should you say? "Excuse me, please."

♥ Don't call people nasty names or make fun of people who are different.

♥ Return things you borrow as soon as you're finished using them.

♥ Be kind to everyone, quick to offer help.

♥ Help an elderly or sick neighbor:

    ♥ Take out the garbage   ♥ Weed the flower beds
    ♥ Feed their pets   ♥ Spend time with them
    ♥ Pick up the mail and
      newspaper

♥ Look for the good in others; overlook the bad.

♥ Don't whisper to your friends in front of others.

♥ Be quiet in public places. There's plenty of time in your day to play. Sometimes you have to be quiet and still.

LIFE LESSON

♥ A Good Sign ♥

A fun and interesting activity to practice common courtesy expressions is to learn how to offer them in different ways. Teach your child how to say thank you, you're welcome, please, excuse me, and I'm sorry in sign language using the diagrams and instructions below.

Demonstrate each movement for your child and practice making the signs together with Wilbur as your teacher.

Please: The open right hand is circled on the chest, over the heart.

PLEASE

Excuse Me, Pardon Me: The right hand is cupped and the tips of the fingers wipe off the left palm several times.

EXCUSE ME

I'm sorry: The right hand made into a fist with the thumb on the outside (the letter "S") and the palm facing the body, is rotated several times over the area of the heart.

I'M SORRY

Thank you: The fingertips of the right hand are placed at the mouth. The hand moves away from the mouth to a palm-up position before the body. Be sure to smile as you sign "thank you."

THANK YOU

You're welcome: Make a W shape with the ring, middle, and index fingers on the right hand. Bring the pinkie and thumb together. Place fingertips at mouth and arc forward and down, ending with palm up.

YOU'RE WELCOME

PLAY BY THE RULES

OBJECTIVE

To teach your child to be honest at all times and play by the rules.

GUIDANCE

> If you can be trusted in
> little things,
> you will be given bigger things.

Share these thoughts with your child:

♥ There is no such thing as a "little white lie." Either you tell the truth or you don't. Being honest in all that you do makes you a child that is trustworthy.

♥ You can't tell just <u>one</u> lie. You'll have to tell another lie to cover the first one.

♥ Don't exaggerate to impress people. Others know when you're "talking big."

♥ If you're told not to do something, then DON'T DO IT! Rules are made to protect you, not to spoil your fun. Rules help you, not hurt you.

♥ Be sure your actions match your words.

♥   If you follow the rules, you will be safe and happy. Learning to "play by the rules" gives you the freedom to have fun without worry.

LIFE LESSON

♥ Wilbur Says ♥

You can play the old game "Simon Says" to reinforce following the rules.   Use the puppet, "Wise Old Wilbur" to call out the commands.   Call the game "Wilbur Says." Wilbur calls out directions such as, "Wilbur says, stand up and turn around."   Your child must follow the directions as long as they begin with "Wilbur says."

DOING YOUR BEST

OBJECTIVE

To teach your child to be responsible in everything they do.

GUIDANCE

> Be the labor great
> or small,
> do it well or not at all🖉

Ask your child if they know what responsibility means. Write their thoughts on a sheet of paper.

Share these thoughts with your child:

♥ Responsibility is a BIG word. It needs to be a BIG word, because it's an important word.

♥ To be responsible means that others can count on you.

♥ Do your best no matter what you're asked to do.

♥ Do your best to be helpful, not to receive a reward.

♥ Being responsible comes from the heart. Your actions show what's in your heart.

♥ Remember at school:

- ♥ Work hard on your assignments.
- ♥ If your teacher asks you to do something extra, do it with a smile and say, "*Yes, Ma'am.*"
- ♥ Take care of your school supplies. Keep up with them. Don't lose them.
- ♥ Accept corrections from your teacher. Learn from your mistakes.

♥ Remember at home:

- ♥ When Mom or Dad asks you to do something, do it immediately.
- ♥ If you tell someone in your family that you'll help them, do it. Don't make excuses to get out of it.
- ♥ Always keep your word.
- ♥ If you've started a tough job, like raking leaves, stay with it. Do a little bit at a time, but don't give up.

LIFE LESSON

♥ The Best Me ♥

Ask your child:

"Do you know what New Year's Resolutions are? They are a list of things people write down before January 1st of the next year that they want to do better. Usually they put things on their list such as, 'I resolve to lose weight' or ' I resolve to give more money to the less fortunate.' We don't need a holiday to make a list of things that we know need improvement. Let's think together of things that we can both improve on in our lives."

With your child make a list of "The Best Me" resolutions. The list will focus mainly on the items covered in this lesson (I.e. "Do your best to be helpful," "Work hard in school," "Always keep your word.")

Photocopy or trace the pattern on the following page. Add your child's resolutions. After it is completed, hang in a prominent place for you and your child to see such as the refrigerator, on the wall in your child's room, etc.

Encourage your child's progress by promising that you too, will work on being "The Best You" that you can be.

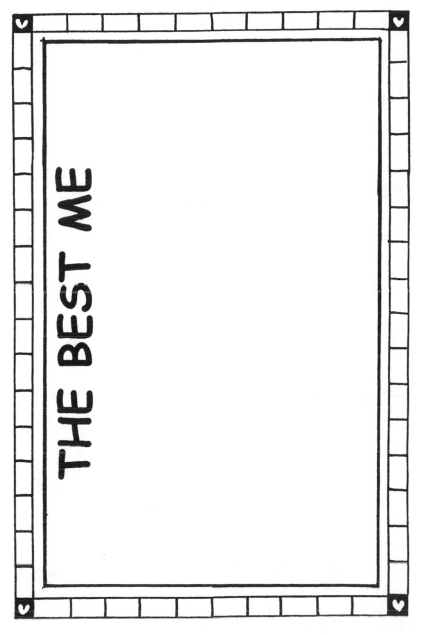

THE BEST ME

I'M SORRY

OBJECTIVE

To teach your child the importance of forgiveness.

GUIDANCE

> We truly must learn to
> forgive and forget.

Share these thoughts with your child:

♥   We've talked about being unselfish and about giving to others.

♥   "*I'm sorry*" are the most unselfish words you can ever offer to someone.

♥   We know when we've been hurt; we feel it in our heart. But, sometimes it's hard to know when we've hurt others.

♥   Forgiveness works in two ways. You need to forgive others and you need to be forgiven.

Ask your child what if:

♥   You lose your temper with your friend and say something ugly? You scream at your mother because she's late for carpool? What should you say?

Give your child an opportunity to answer these questions, then offer these suggestions:

- ♥ You need to say, "I'm sorry. Would you forgive me?"

- ♥ If you are truly sorry for hurting someone's feelings, you won't make excuses for your poor judgement. We all make mistakes, but by admitting your mistake and asking for forgiveness, character is built.

- ♥ When you're truly sorry, you change. When you say, "I'm sorry," what you are really saying is, "I won't do it again."

Ask your child what if:

- ♥ Your friend loses her temper with you and calls you an ugly name? Your brother accidentally steps on your toy and breaks it? What should you say?

Give your child an opportunity to answer these questions, then offer these suggestions:

- ♥ You need to say, "That's okay. I forgive you."

- ♥ When you forgive, you forget about the mistake someone has made and love him or her anyway.

- ♥ Don't hold grudges.

♥   Be quick to forgive.

♥   Forgiveness helps you. When you don't forgive, you have bad feelings that only grow worse until you forgive.

LIFE LESSON

♥ Forgiveness Favor ♥

To make saying "I'm sorry" easier, let's make a Forgiveness Favor.

You'll need two sheets of coordinating tissue paper. Cut into 5" by 7" pieces. (Two standard sheets of tissue will wrap four favors.)

Have your child write the words "I'm sorry" on a slip of paper. (For young children cut out "I'm sorry" slip from the lesson.) Place it inside the roll. Lay the toilet paper roll in the center of the tissue paper.

Mark the ends of the roll on the paper with a pencil. Fringe ends to mark. Wrap paper around roll and seal center with a sticker. Tie both ends with a 6" length of string.

I'M SORRY.

MANNERS OF THE HEART
AT HOME
PART 2

COMMUNICATION

SKILLS

INTRODUCTION

Now that you have established the foundation of goodheartedness in your child, you need to begin adding communication skills. For your child to succeed in the world, he needs to have effective communication skills.

One of the foundations of *Manners of the Heart at Home* is that "respect for one another is the place to start, the rest will come easily." Remember we are raising children to have servant hearts—to be self-giving, not self-serving.

Conveying courtesy and goodheartedness through our speech takes practice and the willingness to learn. This section will give your child the answers to the questions: "What do I say?" and "How do I say it?" It is from this humble confidence, that the child will be able to address adults with respect as "Sir" and "Ma'am."

If you haven't already started taking your children on outings that will challenge and improve their communication skills, this is the time. Encourage your child to be friendly with a quick smile as you visit a nursing home or an elderly relative let your child help make a plate of cookies to take to a neighbor. Invite your child to help you with charitable work in your community. Even a very young child can do simple tasks and will feel great about himself through helping others.

As your child learns how to use the telephone, allow him to answer and place calls in your presence so that you can guide him in practicing this new skill.

As you work through this section, seize every opportunity to put these skills into practice with your child at home and in your community. Helping your child develop communication skills will build self-confidence.

YES, SIR — NO, SIR

OBJECTIVE

To teach your child how to address adults.

GUIDANCE

Share these thoughts with your child.

♥   You want to be remembered as being friendly, not bashful, confident, not shy.

♥   Most of all, you want to be known for being polite and kind-hearted.

♥   Whenever you meet an adult, smile. Meeting new people is exciting, not scary.

♥   Stand tall and don't be shy; look directly into a person's eyes, not around them. You only have one opportunity to make a good first impression. Offer your hand for a firm handshake which is a sign of a confident young person.

♥   When offering your hand for a handshake, remember these tips:

   ♥   Don't let your hand be flimsy;
   ♥   Grip their hand firmly;
   ♥   Don't squeeze too hard.

♥ Never call an adult by their first name. Always use Mr., Mrs., or Miss or a professional title, such as, Doctor, or Reverend.

♥ If an adult asks you to call them by their first name, use Miss or Mr. in front of their name. (E.g. Miss Kris Ann)

♥ Whenever someone enters the room you're in, you should speak. If it is an adult, you should stand as they enter the room.

♥ Always, always use "Yes, Sir/ No, Sir" and "Yes, Ma'am/ No Ma'am" when answering an adult. This shows respect.

LIFE LESSON

♥ Wilbur's Yes Sir, No Sir Bank ♥

Every time your child says yes sir/ma'am, or no sir/ma'am, give him a penny to put in his bank. This is a great way to give your child an extra incentive for helping them develop the habit of speaking properly to adults—a little reward for remembering to practice respectfulness.

What you will need:

Pint milk carton
Construction paper (white, black, red & yellow)
Crayons or Markers
Scissors
Glue

Directions:

A.   Wash and dry pint milk carton.

B.   Cut slots in each side for wings. (Refer to diagram 1 for location.)

C.   Photocopy or trace patterns onto white paper. Glue to construction paper. Color the pictures and cut out.

D.   Fold wing tabs on dotted lines and push wings into slots. From the inside, open tabs to hold the wings in place.

E.   Close the carton top and fasten securely with glue. Clamp with a clothespin until glue dries.

F.   Following the diagram, glue pieces to the front and back of the carton matching head pieces at the top. When the glue is dry, cut coin slot through back vest piece according to pattern.

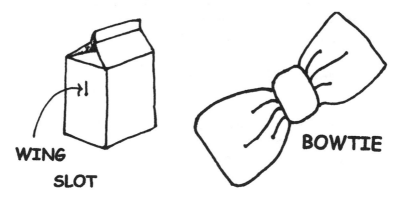

WING

SLOT

DIAGRAM 1

BOWTIE

"WISE OLD WILBUR" BANK

CLAWS

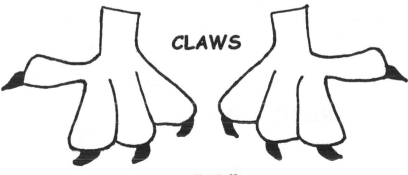

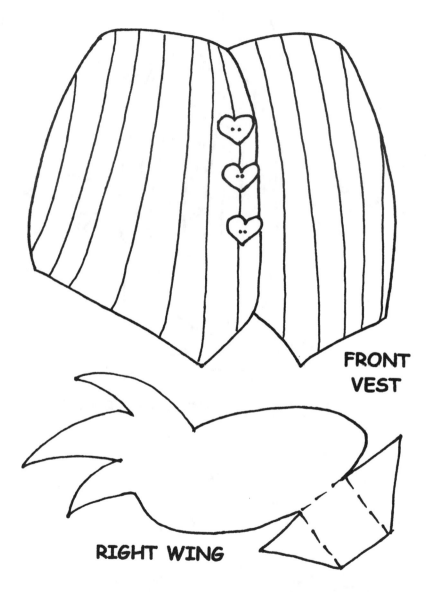

FRONT
VEST

RIGHT WING

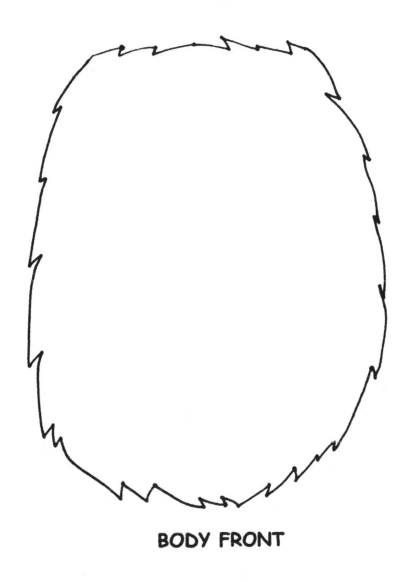

BODY FRONT

HEAD FRONT

HEAD BACK

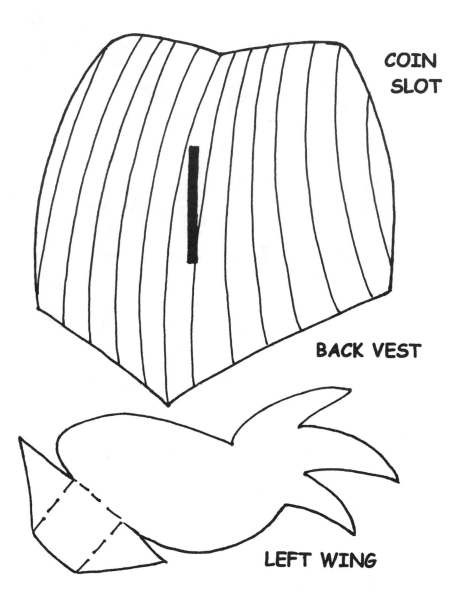

COIN
SLOT

BACK VEST

LEFT WING

HAVE WE MET?

OBJECTIVE

To teach your child how to make proper introductions.

GUIDANCE

Share these thoughts with your child:

♥ Always remember to introduce your new friends to your family. Introduce friends to your family members, using your family member's name first.

♥ When you bring new friends home with you, you should introduce them, this way:

> To Your Mom:
> "Mom, this is Miller Maestri. Miller, this is my Mom, Mrs. Budden."

♥ When your parents visit at school, you should introduce them to your teachers this way:

> To Your Mom and Dad:
> "Mom and Dad, this is my teacher; Mrs. Berry, these are my parents, Randy and Margie Hollis."

♥ When you want a new friend to meet an old friend, you should introduce them this way:

To Your Old Friend:
   "Adam, this is my new friend Brian.
   Brian, this is my friend, Adam."

♥   If you are meeting someone new and no one introduces you, you can introduce yourself.

   Introduce yourself by saying,
      "Hi, (or hello), I'm Hunter Giles, what's your name?"

♥   After you have met someone, a considerate thing to say is, "It was so nice to meet you _____(using his or her name)." This will also help you to remember their name the next time you meet them.

♥   The most important part to remember in meeting new people is to just be you—polite and interested in the new acquaintance.

♥   A simple key to proper introductions is to say the person's name you are closest to or you have known the longest first. (Parent, relative, friend, etc.)

LIFE LESSON

♥ Meet My Toys ♥

Ask the child to bring several stuffed animals or action figures to the area where you're teaching the lesson.

Have the child make introductions to you, using the toys he's brought as new friends.

Example:

"Mom, this is my teddy bear, Mikey Boobear. Mikey, this is my Mom, Mrs. Smith."

"Dad, this is my best toy, Soldier Jim. Jim, this is my Dad, Mr. Barkley."

Make sure that you respond with, "Nice to meet you, Mikey" etc. Take turns making the introductions.

When your child's friends come over to visit, always remind your child to make the proper introductions. The order of introductions is hard to remember. It takes a lot of practice to become confident in this skill. Have patience, use the "general rule" as a reminder—use the name of the eldest person first.

TELEPHONE MANNERS

OBJECTIVE

To teach your child telephone manners.

GUIDANCE

Share these principles with your child for making calls:.

♥ When you make a call let the phone ring several times —six or seven rings— before you hang up.

♥ When someone answers:

   ♥ Speak to the person who answers.
   ♥ Identify yourself.
   ♥ Ask for the person you need to speak with.

♥ If you know the person who answers the phone, be friendly and talk to them for a minute or two.

♥ Don't make a call while you're eating a snack.

♥ Don't talk to someone who is in the same room while you're on the phone. When you're on the phone, give that person your full attention.

♥ If you get a wrong number, don't hang up. Simply say, *"I'm sorry, I must have dialed the wrong number."*

♥ If an answering machine takes your call, leave a short message with the following information:

♥ Your name.
♥ The time you are calling.
♥ A short message.

Share these principles with your child for taking calls:

♥ Whenever you answer the phone, be friendly and speak to the person calling, even if the call is for someone else.

♥ Say "Hello" or "Hello, this is the Jones' residence."

♥ Never answer the phone in a loud voice or by saying "Yeah." Answer in a pleasant, friendly voice.

♥ If the call is for someone not at home, you should say, "I'm sorry, Melissa can't come to the phone right now. May I take a message?"

♥ Keep a pad and paper by the phone to write down messages. If you can't take a message, call someone to the phone that can or suggest that the caller call back in a little while.

♥ If the person calling is a stranger, and your parents are not home, never let them know that you are home alone.

> ♥ If your parent is asked for, say, "Dad isn't available for the phone right now. May I take a message?" or "Mom is busy right now. Could you call back in a little while?"

LIFE LESSON

♥ Cordless Chatter Box ♥

Help your child make two chatterboxes for a fun way to practice making and taking phone calls.

What you will need:

2 boxes approximately 3" x 7" x 2" (A check box works well.)
Construction paper or wrapping paper
Pencil or straw
Scissors
Glue

Directions:

A.   Cover the box in choice of colored paper.

B.   Photocopy or trace telephone pattern on white paper, and glue to construction paper. have your child color the keypad and cut out.

C.   Glue telephone keypad to covered box.

D.   Punch a hole with a small screwdriver through the top of the box for the "antenna." Push pencil or straw through the hole securing with glue.

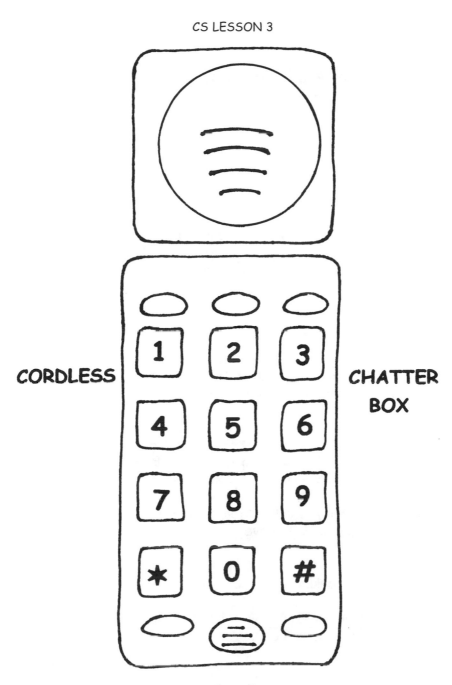

CORDLESS

CHATTER BOX

TALKING AND LISTENING

<u>OBJECTIVE</u>

To teach your child how to be a good conversationalist.

<u>GUIDANCE</u>

> We should listen
> twice as much
> as we talk.

Share these thoughts with your child:

♥   If you want to begin a conversation with someone you've just met, ask a question:

   ♥   Where do you go to school?
   ♥   What's your favorite sport?
   ♥   Have you always lived in Baton Rouge?
   ♥   What's your favorite hobby?

♥   Whenever you talk with someone, young or old, look them directly in the eye.

♥   Try not to look around when you're listening or when you're speaking.

♥   The more questions you ask, the more you will learn about your new friend.

♥ Give a response to what is said. Don't answer questions with just "*yes*" or "*no.*"

♥ Be interested in every word being spoken to you.

♥ There are personal questions you shouldn't ask:

  ♥ "Why are you bald?"
  ♥ "Why are you in a wheelchair?"
  ♥ "How much did that cost?"
  ♥ "Are you rich?"
  ♥ "Do you make good grades?"

♥ Never say anything to hurt another person.

♥ Don't talk about anyone to another person. That's called gossip.

♥ If you ask questions and then listen to the answer, you'll be a favorite friend to a lot of people.

♥ You'll have a lot of time to talk too, if you listen first! Everybody wants someone to listen to them.

♥ Remember your family members have things to share about their day. Ask them questions too!

"HELLO,

AUSTRALIAN: G'Day
(Australia)   Guh day

JAPANESE: Konichiwa
(Japan)   Koh-NEE-cheewah

RUSSIAN: Zdravstvuite
(Russia)   ZzDRAST-vet-yah

SWEDISH: God dag
(Sweden)   Goo dahg

HINDI: Namaste
(India)   Nah-mah-STAY

ITALIAN: Ciao
(Italy)   Chow

HEBREW: Shalom
(Israel)   Sha-LOHM

ARABIC: Marhaba
(Middle East)   Mar-HAH-bah

WORLD!"

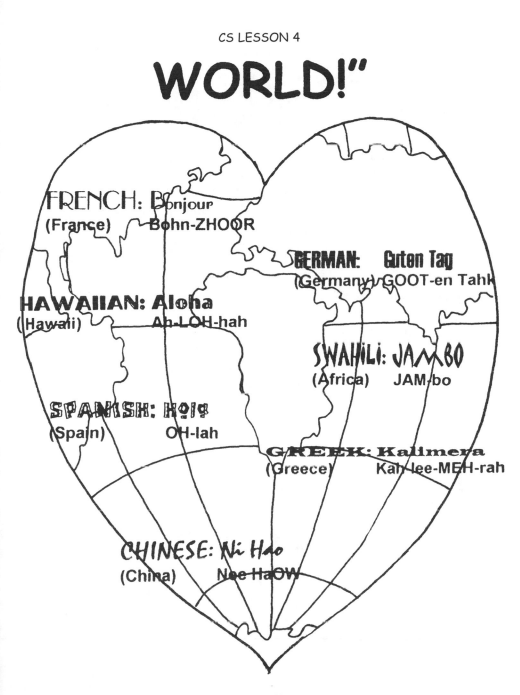

FRENCH: Bonjour
(France)   Bohn-ZHOOR

GERMAN: Guten Tag
(Germany) GOOT-en Tahk

HAWAIIAN: Aloha
(Hawaii)   Ah-LOH-hah

SWAHILI: JAMBO
(Africa)   JAM-bo

SPANISH: Hola
(Spain)   OH-lah

GREEK: Kalimera
(Greece)   Kah-lee-MEH-rah

CHINESE: Ni Hao
(China)   Nee HaOW

LIFE LESSON

♥ Hello, World! ♥

On the previous pages is a list of ways to say hello in different languages. You and your child can enjoy learning the different ways to say hello around the world. Encourage your child to use these new greetings as a great conversation starter.

Example,

Your child: " Ciao, Sarah!"

A friend: "What does that mean?"

Your child: "It means 'hello' in Italian. I know all sorts of ways to say 'hello' in different languages. Would you like to learn?"

A friend: "Yeah, that would be cool."

HAPPY BIRTHDAY

OBJECTIVE

To teach children how to be well-mannered hosts and polite guests at birthday parties.

GUIDANCE

Let's look at both sides of attending a birthday party—as the host and as the guest.

Share these thoughts with your child:

Being a Host:

♥   Greet all guests at the door and introduce them to anyone they don't know. (*Review with your child how to introduce friends to family and new friends to old friends.*)

♥   Be excited about each gift and say a sincere thank you to each guest.

♥   If you receive a gift that you already have, don't say anything that would hurt the giver's feelings. Just say, "Thank you."

♥   If you don't like a gift that you receive, don't let your friend know. Appreciate their thoughtfulness in giving you a gift.

♥ Include everyone in the games. Do your best to see that no one feels left out.

♥ When guests begin to leave, walk each one to the door. Always say thank you for coming to your party and for their gift.

♥ When you meet the birthday child, say an enthusiastic "Happy Birthday" and present them with your gift.

♥ If someone you haven't met is at the door, introduce yourself.

♥ Don't be shy. Join in all the games and activities.

♥ A birthday party is a special occasion when you should really practice your manners.

♥ When you leave, say thank you to your friend and his parents, or hosts, for inviting you to the party.

LIFE LESSON

♥ Silly "Surprise" Party ♥

Throw a silly "surprise" birthday party for a stuffed animal, doll, toy, or even the family pet.

Have fun making invitations that can be hand delivered to other family members and friends.

Party Hats:

A. Cut an 8 ¡ " circle from a sheet of construction paper. Mark the center of the circle.

B. Cut a slit from the outside edge to the center.

C. Wrap the circle into a cone shape and secure the edges together with tape or glue.

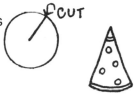

D. Decorate with markers, glitter, picture cutouts, or anything that can be adhered to the hat.

Have your child put one of their toys in a small box to be wrapped and presented as the gift.

Take turns with your child being the host and guest.

♥ Pickapresent ♥

When your child receives an invitation to a birthday party, let him help in choosing the present for the person.

After picking out the present, you and your child can wrap the gift in a fun way, making the gift as special on the outside as it is on the inside.

Here are some suggestions:

♥ Use the colorful Sunday comics as gift-wrap.

♥ Wrap the gift with scraps of fabric.

♥ Have the child make his own wrapping paper using a large sheet of freezer paper. On the "paper side," they can repeat a design, write the recipient's name in different colors or draw a picture. Encourage your child to be creative.

♥ Attach a small toy or trinket to the package near the bow such as a toy car, candy, a personalized item, a stuffed animal, etc.

THANK YOU NOTES

OBJECTIVE

To teach your child the importance of sending thank you notes.

GUIDANCE

Share these thoughts with your child:

♥   A thank you note is a written expression of gratitude from your heart for a kindness extended to you.

♥   Whenever someone takes the time to extend you a kindness, you should write a thank you note.

♥   You should send a thank you note within a few days after receiving the kindness.   Being prompt in responding lets the giver know how much you appreciate your thoughtfulness.

♥   You should write a thank you note for the following occasions:

  ♥   When you've received a gift.
  ♥   When you've been to dinner with a friend.
  ♥   When a kindness has been extended to you.
  ♥   When a gift has come in the mail.

♥   Write more than "thank you." You need to write something interesting about the gift or kindness. This makes the giver feel special.

Example:

> Dear Matt,
>   Thank you for the model car kit.
>   I'm having fun putting it together.
>   Your friend,
>   Chris

♥   Sign your note with Sincerely, Fondly, or Your Friend. Sign your note with Love, if it is a family member, relative or close friend.

LIFE LESSON

♥ Special Delivery ♥

Help your child think of a kindness to be thankful for that a family member has done recently. They may be thankful for the barbecue that Dad grilled last Sunday or the help they received from "Big Sis" with homework. Help them write and mail a thank you note to the family member.

This is a great way to practice writing thank you notes and your child sees the pleasure a thank you note brings to the recipient.

THANK YOU NOTE

VISITING A FRIEND

OBJECTIVE

To teach your child how to use good manners when visiting in someone's home.

GUIDANCE

Share these thoughts with your child:

♥ It's always nice to take a little "happy" to your hostess when you're spending the night.

♥ You can take a flower from your garden or a small gift.

♥ When you enter someone's home, speak to everyone in a friendly voice and introduce yourself.

♥ Remember when we discussed introductions earlier? We discussed introducing yourself by saying "Hi" or "Hello, I'm Laura Birnbaum."

♥ Tell your friend's parents thank you for inviting you over.

♥ Remember to use your "inside voice" at all times.

♥ Don't leave your clothes and shoes lying around. Keep them in one place in your friend's room.

♥ It's not polite to turn on the TV or music without asking permission.

♥   Remember the old saying, "Look, but don't touch."

♥   Be cooperative no matter what is planned at your friend's home. No complaining.

♥   Wait for food to be offered. Never ask for a snack.

♥   Be careful not to splatter water in the bathroom. Help keep it tidy. Hang up your wet towels.

♥   Offer to help in the kitchen before and after meals.

♥   Make up the bed you slept in as soon as you get up.

♥   When it's time to leave, tell your host or hostess thank you again for having you over. Let them know how much you enjoyed the visit. Remember that being a kind guest will help you receive another invitation.

LIFE LESSON

♥ Speedy Sleep-Over ♥

Play a game in which your child pretends she's spending the night at a friend's house.

Help pack a small bag with the items needed for a sleep-over. Have your child make a traditional entrance, just as she would if she were away from home. Remind her to introduce herself and say thank you for the invitation.

Go through a fast paced version of a night at a friend's house—including "dinner," "going to sleep," "getting up" and "going home." Each activity should prompt the child to exhibit a skill she learned in the lesson.

FOR BOYS ONLY

OBJECTIVE

To teach boys the basics of being a gentleman.

GUIDANCE

Share these thoughts with your child:

♥ Webster's dictionary defines gentle as "generous, kind, and patient." To be a gentleman, you must be generous in giving your time to others. You must be kind-hearted toward everyone and patient with your friends, teachers and family.

♥ As a gentleman, it's important to be respectful of ladies. You can show your respectfulness in many ways.

  ♥ Allow ladies to enter and leave an elevator first.

  ♥ Open the entrance and car doors for them

  ♥ Offer to carry heavy packages or books.

  ♥ Help to put on their coats.

  ♥ Pull out their chair for dinner. (This act of kindness brings delight to all ladies, young and old. Always remember to seat your mother, whether at home or in a restaurant.)

  ♥ Get rid of "bathroom talk" — language that discusses bodily functions. This is always inappropriate, especially in the presence of ladies of all ages.

♥ Offer your seat to an elderly lady or man, if all seats are taken in a public place.

♥ When a lady enters a room, or comes to a table where you are seated, you should stand. When a lady stands to leave a room, you should stand.

LIFE LESSON

♥ Maritime Manners Mobile ♥

Help your child make a mobile using nautical symbols that convey the qualities of a respectful gentleman.

What you will need:

2 wire coat hangers
8 (12 inch long) pieces of string or yarn
Twist ties
Markers or crayons
1 (16 oz.) blue or red plastic cup
1 (9 oz.) blue or red plastic cup
Glue
Scissors
Construction paper and plain white paper
1 (35 mm) film canister (black or clear) or similar size container
Hot glue or super glue
Ice pick or sharp object to poke small hole

Making the Mobile:

A. Cross the wire coat hangers to form the mobile frame, placing one hanger (hook pointed upward) through the opening of the other (hook pointed upward). The hanging hooks should meet at the center.

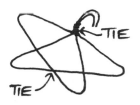

B. Secure the hangers together wrapping twist ties (see above) at the top and bottom where they come into contact.

C. Turn one hook so that it faces the same direction as the other for hanging.

Light of GoodHeartedness Lighthouse:

For this project you will need the 2 cups, construction paper, white paper, glue, hot glue or super glue, scissors and the film canister.

A. Trace or photocopy the beacon pattern onto plain white paper and let the child color the "glow" yellow. Cut out and set aside.

B. Trace or photocopy the guardrail pattern onto plain white paper. Cut out and set aside.

C. Trace the roof circle and door patterns on black construction paper. Cut out and set aside.

D. Trace or photocopy the window patterns on plain white paper. Let your child color the panes yellow. Cut out and set aside.

E. Cut out the "Lighthouse of GoodHeartedness" sign and set aside.

F. To begin construction of the lighthouse, turn the 16 oz. cup upside down. Spread glue around the inner rim of the 9 oz. cup and place on top of the 16 oz cup making the body of the lighthouse. Let dry.

G. Remove the top from the film canister and poke a hole in the center.

H. Spread glue onto the beacon strip and wrap it around the film canister, adhering firmly.

I. Paste the windows and door onto the the cups.

J. Spread glue on the tab of the "Lighthouse of GoodHeartedness" sign and adhere to the side of the larger cup.

K. To make the roof, cut along marked line on pattern. Shape the circle into a cone as shown in the diagram and glue the edges. After drying, poke a small hole in the top to allow the string to go through.

L. Thread the end of the string through the hole in the film canister lid. Tie a stiff and secure knot on the <u>underside</u> of the lid and thread the string through the roof, leaving excess to hang.

M. Hot glue or super glue the film canister to the bottom of the 9 oz. cup. (top of lighthouse) Let dry.

N. Spread glue along long edge of the guard railing and wrap around the top of the lighthouse, so that it stands above the edge of the cup to form the guardrail around the beacon.

O. Cap the film canister to finish the structure and tie the lighthouse to the center of the mobile.

Maritime Manners Symbols:

A. Photocopy the manner's symbols (make 2 copies of each pattern to form fronts and backs). Let your child color and cut the symbols. Match fronts with backs and glue together. Punch a hole at the 'x' for hanging.

B. Thread string through each symbol and tie securely to hangers at points indicated.

C. Shine your light, Mate!

The Lighthouse
of
GoodHeartedness

LIGHTHOUSE SIGN

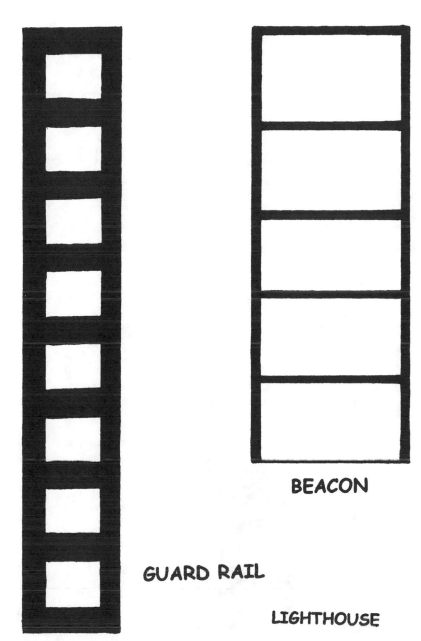

BEACON

GUARD RAIL

LIGHTHOUSE

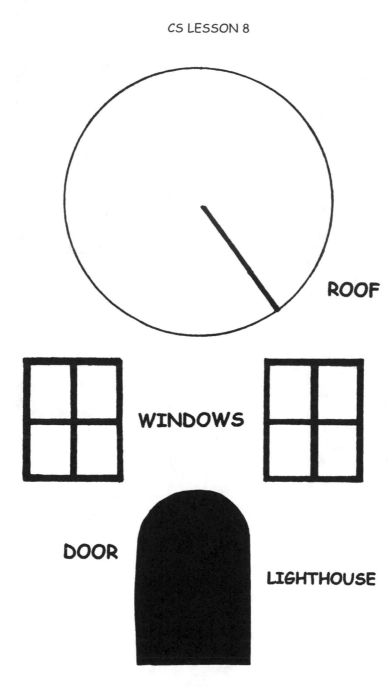

ROOF

WINDOWS

DOOR

LIGHTHOUSE

ANCHOR

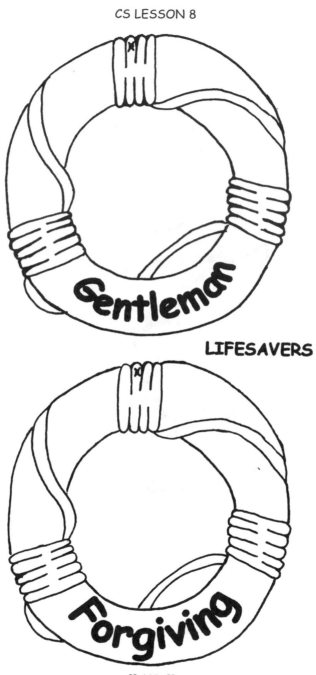

LIFESAVERS

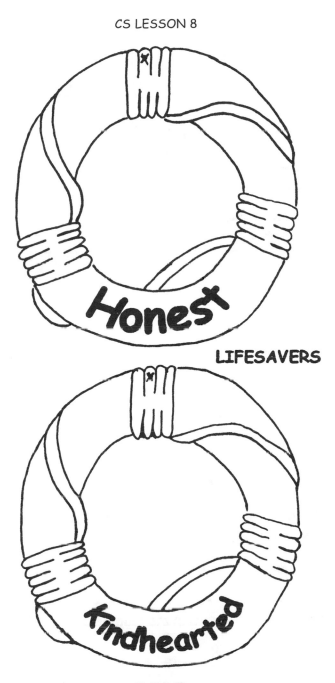

LIFESAVERS

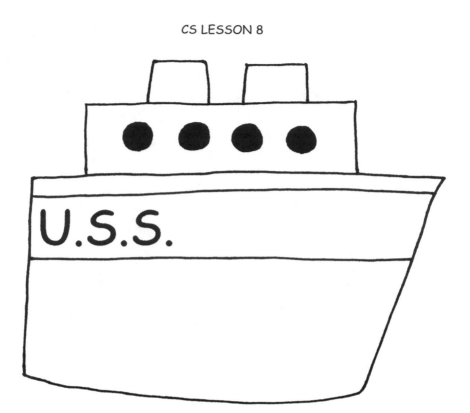

GOODSHIP U.S.S. (your child's name)

Finishing the Mobile:

A. Trace or photocopy the pattern for the lifesavers, anchor and ship.

B. Help your child write his name on the U.S.S. ship.

C. Color and cutout the maritime symbols and tie each to the mobile, as shown in the diagram.

D. Ships Ahoy, Mate!!

FOR GIRLS ONLY

OBJECTIVE

To teach girls the basics of being a lady.

GUIDANCE

Ask your child the following questions:

♥ Have you every heard the expression,
    "Pretty is as pretty does?"

♥ What about,
    "It's not what's on the outside that counts, but what's on the inside?"

Share the following thoughts with your child:

♥ To be treated like a lady, it is important to act like a lady.

♥ If you want boys to treat you with respect, you must act like a lady.

♥ To be a lady, you should:

  ♥ Speak kindly to others.

  ♥ Offer to help others in need.

  ♥ Allow boys to open your door. Wait for your car door to be opened for you. Wait for a gentleman to open a door when entering a building.

♥   Allow boys to pull out your chair at dinner.

♥   To be a lady you should *not*:

   ♥   Say everything that comes to your mind. If you have an ugly thought, keep it to yourself.

   ♥   Sit with your legs open across a chair. Always sit in a chair with your knees together

   ♥ Gossip!

   ♥ Use ugly words

♥   Practice being a good hostess at home. Help your mom when company comes over.

♥   When your friends come for a visit, offer them refreshments. Serve your friends.

LIFE LESSON

♥ Hearts in Hand ♥

The "Heart in Hand" sign is a Shaker symbol that originated in the 1700's, which meant "Hands to work and Hearts to God." Today, it's also recognized as a symbol of friendship and sharing.

Help your child construct a mobile using the "Heart in Hand" symbol surrounded by hearts.

What you will need:

2 wire coat hangers
5 (12 inch long) pieces of ribbon
Twist ties
Markers or poster paint
Salt dough recipe
Toothpick
Sharp knife or heart-shaped cookie cutter

Heart in Hand sculpture:

You will need 1cup flour, 1 cup salt, and 1/4 cup water.

A.   Mix together the flour, salt and half the water in a mixing bowl. Knead dough, gradually adding the rest of the water until the dough is smooth and firm. Don't add the water too quickly or you'll end up with a sticky mess!

B.   Roll out the dough to ¡ inch thickness on wax paper. Ask your child to lay her hand flat on the dough with fingers together. Use a toothpick to trace around the edge of her hand.

C.   Lift her hand and draw lines for fingers.

D.   Cut a heart shape out of the center of the hand using a sharp knife or a cookie cutter. Poke a hole at the tip of the middle finger for hanging.

E.   Place the sculpture on a sheet of cardboard and let dry overnight until hardened.

F. Cut out twelve heart shapes from construction paper using the small, medium and large patterns, cutting four from each size. Help your child write the names of her friends or loved ones on the paper hearts with a marker or paint pen. On a few hearts, write the attributes of goodheartedness such as, kindness, patience, etc. Punch holes in each for hanging.

G. After the "Heart in Hand" sculpture is dry and hardened designs may be added with poster paint or markers. You can use the heart "window" in the hand as a tiny picture frame. Your child may want to put her best friend's photo or one of herself inside. Secure the photo in place with tape and glue a piece of construction paper behind the photo to hold in place.

Making the Mobile:

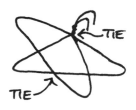

A. Cross the wire coat hangers to form the mobile frame, placing one hanger (hook pointed upward) through the opening of the other (hook pointed upward). The hanging hooks should meet at the center.

B. Secure the hangers together wrapping twist ties at the top and bottom where they come into contact. (See diagram above).

C. Turn one hook so that it faces the same direction as the other for hanging.

D.   Thread one end of yarn through the hanging hole in each heart and knot to secure. Tie the "Heart in Hand" sculpture to the center of the mobile.

E.   Tie the four hanging hearts on each corner of the mobile.

F.   Hearts in Hand!

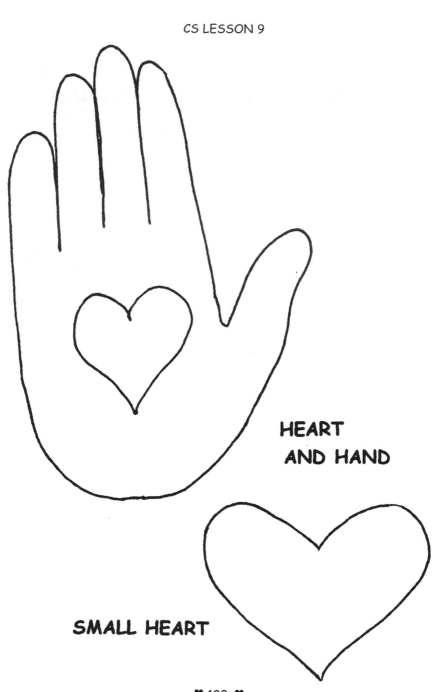

HEART
AND HAND

SMALL HEART

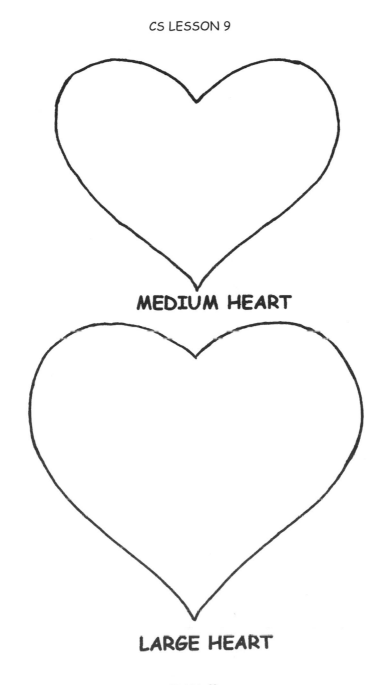

MEDIUM HEART

LARGE HEART

MANNERS OF THE HEART
AT HOME
PART 3

TABLE

MANNERS

INTRODUCTION

Let's begin teaching table manners! "The rules of etiquette" encompass everything from putting a napkin in the lap to saying, "May I be excused, please?" before leaving the table.

I know you've been waiting for the "secret answer" to the question posed on the back cover: "How do we teach our children if we didn't learn all that stuff ourselves?" The proven method for teaching these skills is:

REPETITION, NOT DISCIPLINE!

Let me share a personal story that illustrates this method of teaching manners from the days when I was attempting to guide my children:

One night Boyce, one of my precious six-year-olds, had just put the last bit of macaroni and cheese in his mouth. He jumped up from the table and headed to the playroom to finish his latest Lego® creation.

I said, "Now, wait a minute. Did you forget something? Remember what we do before we leave the table? Back up and give me ten."

"Aww, Mom," he replied.

Scowling, he returned to the table to finish his dinner the proper way—ten times!!!

Holding his dinner plate, he asked, "May I be excused, please?"

I replied, "Yes, you may."

He stood up with dishes in hand, walked to the sink and placed them in the basin. Sighing, he reached in and picked them up again, then turning with an exasperated huff, he returned to the table and sat down.

He began again, "May I ...."

Then I replied, "Yes, you may."

By his third request, his brother Chad, his dad and I began to giggle. Soon Boyce's scowl turned into a sheepish grin, and he broke into boisterous laughter.

By the tenth time, I could barely stammer, "Yes, you may." The family was in stitches.

The lesson learned from this silly event was never forgotten by anyone at the table that night.

I know this method takes time and patience on the part of the adult in charge, but as you can see this exercise becomes fun after a few repetitions. Your family too, will probably develop a case of the giggles as you use this process. Through the years as other parents have used this approach to teaching manners, they have reported great success as well. It may take more than one attempt, but rarely does it take more than three separate attempts for a child to remember the lesson being taught.

As you teach table manners, remember that children learn better without the use of "DON'T! DON'T! DON'T!" Instead, give them their "DO'S!" Rephrase your commands.

Rather than saying,
   "Don't chew with your mouth open,"
   say "Please chew with your mouth closed."

Instead of saying,
   "Don't put your elbows on the table,"
   say, "Keep your elbows at your sides, please."

Designate one mealtime a week for teaching and practicing manners called "Manners Night." In setting aside a special time to practice manners, you will eliminate the need to act as "Manners Police" at every meal. Mealtime will become a pleasant experience for the whole family as everyone develops confidence in their etiquette skills. At the conclusion of this part of the book, we offer helpful suggestions for making "Manners Night" in your home a success.

This is how we teach our children all that "stuff" we didn't learn ourselves. (Now, we can finally learn it, too!)

NAPKIN IN LAP

OBJECTIVE

To teach your child how to properly use his napkin.

GUIDANCE

The first task when you are
seated at the table is put the
napkin in your lap.

Let your child practice using their napkin, as you demonstrate how to use both a paper and cloth napkin:

♥ If you are given a paper napkin, open it, fold it in half. Place it on your lap with folded edge toward your body.

♥ If you are given a cloth napkin, fold it by one-third. Place it on your lap with folded edge toward your body.

♥ The reason for folding your napkin this way is to allow you to blot your mouth without staining your clothing.

♥ To use your napkin, lift the edge to your mouth and gently touch your lips.

♥   If you must leave the table during the meal, place your napkin loosely folded on your chair so others are not viewing a soiled napkin on the table.

♥   When the meal is finished, loosely fold your napkin and put it at the left of your place on the table.

LIFE LESSON

♥ Classic Restaurant Fold ♥

Have your child try a basic napkin fold, "The Classic Fold." Paper or cloth napkins can be used.

Help your child fold his napkin by working through the step by step instructions. They are illustrated on the following page.

1. Fold napkin in half to form a triangle.
2. Fold tip of triangle into the middle.
3. Fold remaining sides down, creating a smaller square.
4. Fold flaps behind creating a triangle.
5. Fold the napkin along center to create a classic restaurant fold.

This is a fun fold to learn, because your children can set the table just like they do in the restaurants!

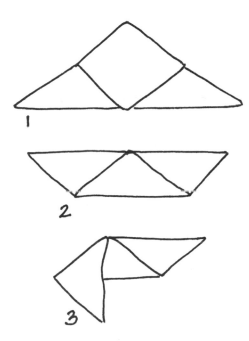

1

2

3

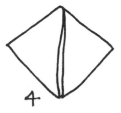

4

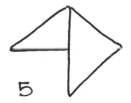

5

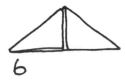

6

SIT UP STRAIGHT

OBJECTIVE

To teach your child the importance of good posture at the dinner table.

GUIDANCE

Let your child practice sitting up straight, as you demonstrate

♥ Sit up straight with your feet on the floor.

♥ Don't slouch at dinnertime. It makes it harder to properly digest your food.

♥ Sit still and keep your hands and feet to yourself.

♥ Don't lean the chair back on its legs. The legs could snap or, even worse, *you* could snap and land on the floor.

♥ Bring the food to your mouth without slumping over your plate. Hold your food over your plate, as you eat, taking care not to lean too far forward.

♥ Never wrap your free arm around the dinner plate while you are eating.

♥ The hand not being used for eating should stay in your lap.

BEING THANKFUL

OBJECTIVE

To teach your child to be thankful before every meal.

GUIDANCE

Share the following thoughts with your child:

♥   The dinner table is a place to remember how fortunate you are to be provided for. It is important to pause before you begin eating to be appreciative for the food and to acknowledge the world around you. Whether at home or in a restaurant, always remember to pause and be thankful for the meal set before you.

♥   When you are the guest of another family, be respectful of their traditions. Many families and individuals say a blessing aloud before their meal. Wait for a blessing to be offered before you begin.

♥   Some families hold hands around the table, fold their hands at the edge of the table, or keep their hands in your lap for the blessing.

LIFE LESSON

♥ Blessings ♥

On the following page are samples of blessings. You may ask your child to memorize one of the poems to say at dinner tonight.

We are thankful for happy hearts,
For rain and sunny weather.
We are thankful for this, our food, and that
We are together.

Adapted from a poem by Emille Fendall Johnson

♥

We are thankful for this food,
For rest and home and all things good;
For wind and rain and sun above,
But most of all for those we love.

Adapted from a poem by Mary Leona Frost

♥

For every cup and plateful,
We are truly grateful.

Adapted from a poem by A.S.T. Fisher

WATCH YOUR ELBOWS

OBJECTIVE

To teach your child to be aware of their elbows at the table.

GUIDANCE

The old saying,
"Elbows off the table"
still holds true today.

Share the following principles with your child:

♥ When you are eating, never prop your elbows on the table.

♥ Keep your elbows close to your side at all times during a meal. Your arms shouldn't look like a butterfly in flight when cutting food.

♥ When talking, be careful not to "poke" your neighbor at the table with your elbow. Keep your arms as still as possible during a conversation.

♥ Between courses, and when you are not eating, you may rest your forearm on the edge of the table.

♥ Once you have completed your meal and the dishes have been cleared, you can prop your elbows on the table.

USING THE FORK

OBJECTIVE

To teach your child how to use a fork properly.

GUIDANCE

Show your child the following principles using a fork and plate:

♥ Use your fork to determine the right size for a bite of food. It should be the size of the prongs of your fork.

♥ After you pierce a bite of food with your fork, eat it. Don't wave it in the air while you're talking between bites.

♥ You should scoop vegetables with your fork, rather than pierce them. Foods such as meats and chicken can be pierced.

♥ You may use a small piece of bread or the tip of your knife to push small bits of food on to your fork.

♥ Always put your fork on your plate between bites. Be careful not to hold it in your hand while talking and drinking. Never put a used fork on the table. Always place it on your plate in a clear spot not on top of uneaten food.

♥ Always work from the outside in when deciding which utensil to use for your meal. (i.e. The salad is served first, so you will find the salad fork on the outside of the place setting.)

CHOP, CHOP

OBJECTIVE

To teach your child the correct way to cut food.

GUIDANCE

Show and tell these principles to your child using a knife, fork and plate.

♥   Hold the knife in your right hand with forefinger extended, resting on the handle to help apply pressure while cutting.

♥   Hold the fork in your left hand, prongs down, to pierce the piece of food. Be careful when holding the utensils not to wrap your hand around the handle.

♥   Cut one or two pieces at a time. Never cut the entire serving of food all at once. After cutting, lay the knife across the rim of your dinner plate.

♥   Some foods, such as pies, cakes and vegetables, can be cut with your fork.

♥   Salad greens can be cut into bite-sized pieces using your knife and fork.

FULL MOUTH

OBJECTIVE

To teach your child what to do when their mouth is full.

GUIDANCE

Share the following principles with your child:

♥ Chew with your mouth closed. Eat small bites, chewing each piece well.

♥ Eat quietly. No smacking, licking your lips or gurgling noises, as you chew or swallow.

♥ Never talk with your mouth full.

♥ If you already have food in your mouth, don't take a drink to "wash it down." After you have swallowed the food, take a sip or two of your beverage.

♥ If a piece of gristle needs to be removed from your mouth, you may gently push it from your mouth to a fork and place it on the edge of your plate. Never spit anything into your napkin.

♥ If a bite of food is too hot, quickly take a sip of water. If this doesn't relieve you, remove the bite of food from your mouth and place it on your plate.

COUGHING AND SNEEZING

OBJECTIVE

To teach your child how to be considerate of others when coughing or sneezing at the table.

GUIDANCE

Share the following principle with your child:

♥ When you feel a cough or sneeze coming on, immediately turn your head to the side and away from the table. If you do not have a handkerchief, cover your mouth with your napkin. Don't be tempted to use your sleeve instead. If you're sitting between two people, turn your head to the back of your chair.

♥ If you need to blow your nose, say to your host or hostess or the person sitting closest to you, "Excuse me, please." Never use your napkin to blow your nose. Leave the room and find a restroom to blow your nose. Don't forget to wash your hands before returning to the table.

♥ If you have a bout of coughing that persists, excuse yourself from the table.

♥ If you accidentally burp, don't make any remarks or funny comments. Quietly say, "Excuse me."

EATING SOUP

OBJECTIVE

To teach your child the correct way to eat soup.

GUIDANCE

Share the following principles with your child. Use a soup bowl, soupspoon, and plate to demonstrate.

♥   Wait a few minutes before eating, if the soup is steaming hot. Don't blow on it to cool it. You may skim the top to enjoy a small taste to check for the temperature of the soup.

♥   NO SLURPING.

♥   Eat from the side of the soupspoon or the tip, but don't put the whole spoon in your mouth. (*You could show a soupspoon and a dinner spoon, so that the child can see how much larger a soupspoon is.*)

♥   Always move the spoon in the bowl away from you when eating soup so that if it spills, it won't land in your lap.

♥   Soup served in a cup is eaten with a spoon, until the last few sips. You can drink the rest. Be careful to remove the spoon before lifting the cup to drink.

♥   If necessary, tilt the bowl slightly, away from you, to retrieve the last taste of soup.

♥   If you have an under plate, leave the spoon on it when not eating. If there is no under plate, leave the spoon in your bowl.

♥   When you have finished your soup, leave the spoon on the under plate. If you don't have an under plate, leave the spoon in the center of your bowl.

PASS THE PEAS, PLEASE

OBJECTIVE

To teach your child how to pass food at the table.

GUIDANCE

Share the following principles with your child:

♥   You can reach across for what you need, such as salt and pepper, as long as you don't stretch across your neighbor's place at the table.

♥   If you need something that is out of reach, ask the person sitting next to you, "Would you please pass the sugar?"   When the needed item it passed to you, always say, "Thank you."

♥   When food is passed, it should move from person to person.   When the breadbasket comes to you, hold it with one hand, reach in and take the roll or slice closest to you.   Never touch other rolls, only the one you pick up for yourself.   Don't "pick over" all the pieces, looking for the biggest piece.   This is true also for plates of hors d'oeuvres, cookies, etc.

♥   When passing any serving piece with a handle, pass it with the handle facing the person receiving the serving piece.

♥   When a vegetable bowl is passed, always use the serving utensil provided with the bowl.   Don't use your utensil. Be careful to pass the serving utensil with the bowl.

♥ Sometimes eyes can be bigger than our stomachs. However, don't take more than you can eat.

♥ When passing your plate to receive a second helping, leave your knife and fork in the center of your plate so that they do not fall.

♥ Food is always passed from left to right, counter-clockwise.

BREAD, BUNS AND ROLLS

OBJECTIVE

To teach your child the correct way to eat bread.

GUIDANCE

Share the following principles with your child:

♥ Remember that when the breadbasket comes to you, hold it with one hand, reach in and take the roll or slice closest to you. If a basket of rolls is passed take only one. Never touch other rolls, only the one you pick up for yourself.

♥ Always place your serving of bread on the bread and butter plate or if not provided, on your dinner plate. Never on the table or tablecloth.

♥ If an uncut loaf of bread is passed at the table, break off a serving for yourself. Be courteous to those at your table by only taking what you can eat.

♥ When butter is passed in a stick on a butter dish, cut a small pat from one end with your clean butter knife or dinner knife, if a butter knife is not provided, and place it on your bread and butter plate.

♥ Break a bite-sized piece from your roll. Then, hold the piece on the edge of your plate and spread enough butter for one bite.

♥   If you're eating toast or a hot biscuit, you can butter the whole piece so that butter can melt and then break bite size pieces as you eat.

CHICKEN, SPAGHETTI AND STUFF

OBJECTIVE

To help your child learn how to eat foods that can be awkward to handle.

GUIDANCE

Share the following principles and thoughts with your child:

♥ Some foods have different rules for eating, depending on where you are dining.

♥ Fried chicken and French fries served at the dinner table, should be eaten with a fork, but when served at a picnic, can be eaten with your fingers.

♥ Bacon that's crisp can be eaten with your fingers, but it it's limp, it should be cut and eaten with a fork.

♥ Fresh fruit cut into pieces should be eaten with a fork. Strawberries that have a dip served with them, can be held by the stem, dipped in sugar or glaze and then eaten.

♥ A banana at the dinner table is peeled, cut into bite sized pieces and eaten with a fork.

♥ Barbecue meats, such as ribs, can be pulled apart and eaten with fingers.

♥ Corn on the cob is eaten with the fingers. It's all right to butter the whole cob while it is still hot so the butter can melt.

♥ Spaghetti can be cut into small pieces or it can be eaten by twirling a few strands around your fork while holding the fork against the edge of your plate or a large spoon.

OOPS! SPILLS

OBJECTIVE

To teach your child how to handle spills.

GUIDANCE

Share the following thoughts with your child:

Spills will happen. Here are a few tips on how to handle them:

♥ If you drop a utensil on the floor at home or in anyone's home, pick it up, lay it aside and ask for another. In a restaurant, leave the utensil on the floor and ask the waiter for another.

♥ If you spill a little water on the table, use you napkin to gently pat it dry. If you have a major spill of a beverage, apologize to your hostess and offer to help clean it up.

♥ If you drop a bit of food on the table, simply scoop it up with your spoon or knife and put it on the edge of you plate. If it caused a stain, dab a little water on it with your napkin. Let your hostess know at the end of the meal about the stain.

♥ Never feel embarrassed about a spill. It can happen to anyone.

♥   After the spill is cleaned up, forget about it. The less you make a fuss about it, the less others will remember.

TABLE TALK

OBJECTIVE

To teach your child appropriate conversation at the table.

GUIDANCE

Share the following principles with your child:

♥　When food is passed or offered that you don't like, take a small portion anyway.　Never ask what it is or question the hostess about "gross-looking" stuff.

♥　Try new foods that are offered.　You never know when you might find a new favorite food.

♥　You don't have to eat everything on your plate, but don't complain about the food that has been placed before you.

♥　If you taste a food that's really awful to you, simply try to swallow it.　Don't shout out, "Yuck!"　Take a small sip of water to help wash it down.　If you can't, remember the lesson on removing food from your mouth onto a fork and place it on the edge of your plate.　Do it quietly, without saying a word.

♥　If you really like a dish, say so.　Let the hostess know how much you enjoyed a particular food.

♥　Don't talk about "gross" stuff during a meal.　Ask others what's going on in their lives.　Good conversation starts with questions like, "What did you do today, Mom?" or "Sis, was your English test hard today?"

♥   Use your "inside" voice at the table.

♥   Don't talk about anyone's habits or dress at the table.

♥   You can offer to help serve the food and clean up after the meal, by saying:

    ♥ "May I help with supper, Mrs. Munson?"
    ♥ "I'll be glad to help with the dishes, Mrs. Lunceford."

PLEASE, THANK YOU

OBJECTIVE

To remind your child to be appreciative and polite at the table.

GUIDANCE

Share the following thoughts with your child:

♥ Do you remember the three magic words we talked about earlier? They are "thank you," "please" and "excuse me." You should use all of these at every meal. Here are some examples:

♥ When asking someone to pass something to you, you should say, "Would you pass the ketchup, please?" When the ketchup is passed to you, you should say "thank you."

♥ If you need to leave the table during the meal, you should say, "May I be excused, please?"

♥ These are called the "magic" words, because when you use them, they change a command into a request.

♥ Every time you make a request of your hostess, say, "please." When she takes care of your need, always say, "thank you."

♥ If you accidentally burp at the table say, "Excuse me, please."

WHEW! IT'S OVER

OBJECTIVE

To help your child understand what to do before leaving the table.

GUIDANCE

Share the following principles with your child:

Before leaving the table, you need to remember a few important rules:

♥　Place your napkin gently folded on the left of your place at the table. Don't crumple it; just lay it on the table.

♥　Always say thank you to the host or hostess for preparing the meal. It's especially nice to offer a compliment, such as, "I enjoyed my dinner" or "You're a great cook." (*But be sincere.*)

♥　Before leaving the table, ask the host or hostess if you may be excused by saying, "May I be excused, please?" Whether at home or visiting in a friend's home, offer to clean up and take your plate to the counter by the sink.

♥　When you leave the table, remember to push your chair back under the table.

♥   Place the knife and fork across the center of the plate face down, parallel to each other and the edge of the table, before picking up your plate.

SETTING THE TABLE

OBJECTIVE

To teach your child how to set the table for a family meal.

GUIDANCE

Show your child how to properly set the table using a placemat, two glasses, teaspoon, soupspoon, fork and spoon for dessert, dinner knife, dinner fork, salad fork, dinner plate, salad plate, bread and butter plate, and a napkin.

♥   Put the dinner plate in the center of the placemat. You will build the table setting around the dinner plate.

♥   Add the silverware. Let me give you an easy way to remember which side of the plate to place silverware.

♥   The word FORK has four letters; the word LEFT has four letters.

♥   The words KNIFE and SPOON have five letters; the word RIGHT has five letters.

♥   So, the forks go on the left and the knives and spoons go on the right.

♥   Begin with the dinner knife by placing it next to the dinner plate with the sharp edge facing the plate.

♥ The teaspoon is placed to the right of the knife. If an iced teaspoon is used, it is placed to the right of the teaspoon. Next to the teaspoon is the soupspoon.

♥ Now, move to the left of the dinner plate. The dinner fork is placed closest to the plate. The salad fork is placed to the left of the dinner fork.

♥ The dessert silverware is placed above the plate. Place a fork above the plate with the handle pointing to the right. If you also need a spoon, place it above the fork with the handle pointing to the left.

♥ Now, the silverware is in place. Check the line of the silverware across the bottom to be sure it is even.

♥ Now add the additional plates. The bread and butter plate belongs at the top of the forks. The salad plate is placed below the bread and butter plate and to the left of the forks.

♥ Add the glassware. If only one glass is used, place it above the tip of the knife. If additional glasses are used, such as tea and water, the water glass always sits at the tip of the knife and the second glass is placed to the right of the water glass.

♥ The final touch is the napkin. There are many ways to fold the napkin. The simplest everyday fold is to fold the napkin in half, and half again and then again. Place the folded napkin in one of three places.

   1. In the center of the dinner plate.

   2. To the left of the place setting.

3. On the bread and butter plate.

♥   Remember to always work from the outside in when deciding which utensil to use for your meal. (e.g. The salad is served first, so you will find the salad fork on the outside of the place setting.)

EATING OUT

OBJECTIVE

To help you child learn the "extra" rules of dining out.

GUIDANCE

For girls:

Wait for a young man to pull out your chair and seat you at the table. Say "thank you" to the gentleman who seats you.

For boys:

Assist ladies with their chairs. Walk behind each lady's chair and say, "May I get your chair?" Then, gently pull the chair from the table and wait for the lady to be seated. Slowly slide the chair with her as she sits down.

Share the following principles with your child:

♥   First and foremost, sit still and speak quietly at the table. Use your "inside" voice at all times.

♥   If there are crackers at the table, you may eat a cracker or two. Place the wrappers under the edge of the bread and butter plate.

♥   If you are ordering for yourself, make up your mind quickly and speak clearly to the waiter. Don't let your eyes get bigger than your stomach; order only what you can eat.

♥ Each time the waiter brings anything to the table, say, "Thank you." Say, "please" each time you make a request.

♥ Don't play with the ketchup, sugar or the salt and pepper. Think about how you would feel if you tired to use the peppershaker and the lid fell off spilling pepper on your food.

♥ At the end of the meal, place the knife and fork across the center of the plate, with the sharp edge of the knife pointing down and the tines of the fork laying face down. This signals the waiter that you're finished.

♥ You need to stay seated until everyone has finished his or her meal. If you finish before everyone else, sit quietly and enjoy the conversation.

♥ Keep your napkin in your lap until you are ready to leave the table. Then lay it, gently folded, at the left side of your place as you stand to leave the table.

♥ Remember all the table manners that we've already discussed in previous lessons.

LIFE LESSON

♥ Out to Eat ♥

For a special treat, take your child out to a restaurant to practice his skills.

♥ Maison Manners ♥

Another fun and inexpensive way to give your child the dining out experience is to create your own little "restaurant" at home. Make menus using the sample menu on the following page. Family members can take turns playing waiter or waitress using a pad and pencil to take orders. Young children might need assistance from an older child or adult with serving the meal. Remind the "waiters" to serve the plates from the left and remove them from the right. For extra fun, distribute play money to everyone for paying his or her "bill."

After practicing this activity several times, invite guests to join your family for a meal at Maison Manners so your children can demonstrate their skills.

HEART'S CAFÉ MENU

♥ ♥ ♥

APPETIZERS

- ♥ Etiquette Enchiladas
- ♥ No Slurp Soup
- ♥ Peter Pumpkin Soup

SANDWICHES

- ♥ Smiley Burger
- ♥ Friendly Fish Sandwich

ENTREES

- ♥ Wilbur's Fried Chicken
- ♥ Pork Chop, Chop
- ♥ Cut-n-Twirl Spaghetti
- ♥ Butterfly Beef Wellington

SIDE ORDERS

- ♥ Golden Fried Corn Cakes
- ♥ Honest Onion Rings
- ♥ Good-Hearted Potatoes

DESSERTS

- ♥ Penelope's Tapioca Pudding
- ♥ Happy Cake
- ♥ Forgiveness Fudge

BEVERAGES

- ♥ Lady Bug Punch
- ♥ Cheerful Cherry Shake
- ♥ MeMe's Milk

1234 Respect Road
Happyville, USA

For take out orders
555-6789

MANNERS NIGHT

This is an opportunity to help your children practice the lessons that you've been teaching. Understanding that families lead busy lives, with hectic schedules, I know that it will be difficult to set aside this time. I can assure you that it will be well worth it. To spend an hour or less, one night a week working on manners will eliminate the need to constantly correct your children at every meal. Don't be surprised if this becomes the family's favorite meal of the week.

Here are several suggestions which will make "Manners Night" a fun learning experience:

Preparation:

♥ During the week your child can have fun making special place cards and placemats to be used on "Manners Night."

♥ Plan menus that will enable everyone to practice their etiquette skills such as spaghetti, steak, fried chicken, etc. Allow family members to take turns choosing their favorite foods from your menus.

♥ Let your child be creative by making a centerpiece. (i.e. A grouping of their favorite toys, a vase full of flowers picked from the yard or handmade paper flowers, a stack of blocks, a Lego® sculpture, etc.)

♥ Encourage your child to practice setting the table and making the Classic napkin fold.

♥ Remind your family to come to the table with a neat and tidy appearance. No caps allowed!!

♥ For a special touch, eat by candlelight.

During the Meal:

♥ For maximum benefit, turn off the television.

♥ Encourage everyone at the table to mind their "P's" and "Q's."

♥ Remember it's better to instruct with "DO'S" instead of "DON'TS."

♥ Discipline is inappropriate during "Manners Night," use repetition instead.

After the Meal:

♥ On this night, no one should leave the table until everyone is finished.

♥ Remind your family to place their napkin, loosely folded, to the left of their place setting.

♥ Remember Boyce's story. You must first ask to be excused before leaving the table with your dishes.

♥ Remind your family to say "thank you" to the "chef of the evening."

CHECK LIST

- ♥   Set the table properly.

- ♥   "May I take your hat?"

- ♥   Gentleman, young and old, seat the ladies.

- ♥   Napkin on lap!

- ♥   Keep good posture.

- ♥   Bless the food.

- ♥   Elbows at sides.

- ♥   Mind your utensils.

- ♥   Pass with care.

- ♥   One roll please.

- ♥   Chew with your mouth closed.

- ♥   Use good table talk!

- ♥   Say "Please" and "Thank You."

- ♥   "May I be excused, please?"

- ♥   Put your chair under the table.

P.S.

I encourage you to continue gently reminding your children of these lessons. Please don't become disheartened if at times there seems to be little evidence of all that you've been teaching. As you train your child in goodheartedness, these seeds *will* grow, little by little. It takes time, and no matter the age, we all forget our "P's" and "Q's" sometimes.

At seventeen, our boys have memory lapses from time to time and I have to remind them to open the car door or say "Thank you." In turn, when I have too much to say, they take great pleasure in reminding me not to interrupt their sentences or talk with my mouth full. (Ouch!)

When you sow the seeds of goodheartedness in your child, he will reap the benefit of self-respect. Remember **REPETITION AS A DISCIPLINE** is the most effective method of teaching these life skills. As you reinforce these lessons by modeling them in your own life, your children will develop confidence in following in your footsteps.

This is a joyful, lifelong process because you are passing on to the next generation the

Manners
of YOUR
Heart

How do you plant the seeds
of
Good Heartedness?

Through **R**epetition,

Example and

Sacrifice.

With **P**atience and

Earnestness to meet

the **C**hallenge

of **T**raining our children.

About the Author

JILL RIGBY is an accomplished speaker, columnist, television personality, family advocate, and founder of Manners of the Heart Community Fund, a nonprofit organization bringing a return of civility and respect to our society. Whether equipping parents to raise responsible children, encouraging the education of the heart, or training executives in effective communication skills, Jill's definition of manners remains the same—an attitude of the heart that is self-giving, not self-serving. She is the proud mother of twin sons who testify to her contagious passion.

Others Are Saying. . .

"*Manners of the Heart is a wonderful tool. I believe it is one of the best — **if not the best social skills** curriculum I have used during my 20 years as an educator. Children look forward to the lessons and they're remembering and using the common courtesies they've been taught.*"

Mary Young, Counselor, Head Elementary

"*I am delighted with Manners of the Heart. It is a desperately needed program. I do trust that it will be eagerly received by thousands...*"

Elisabeth Elliot, Speaker and Author

"*Finally, we're 'speaking the right language.' Everyone, even grandparents and the PTA, is involved with Manners of the Heart. The letter below is just one example of how happy parents are with this curriculum. It's making a big difference in our school—we know it will have a lifelong positive impact on our students and their families!*"

McKenzie, Principal, Dozier Elementary

"*The lesson activities are great! Based on 'putting others before yourself,' child-ren really enjoy giving their handmade crafts to brothers and sisters and friends.*"

Judy Powell, Teacher, Vaughn Road Elementary

Manners of the Heart Community Fund

Manners of the Heart is a nonprofit organization working to bring a return of respect and civility to our society through curricula for K-12 students, parenting seminars, and high-impact training for corporations and communities.

Manners of the Heart Curriculum

Can you imagine how different our society would be if every child had self-respect and showed respect for others? Our elementary school curriculum makes it possible. Through the use of creative materials, intensive training for educators and parents, and support from volunteers, *Manners of the Heart* brings schools, homes, and communities together to prepare young people with not only head knowledge but heart knowledge to lead in the right direction.

The Business *of* Manners™

Leading from the heart.

The Business of Manners Seminar

From the fine art of the handshake, the importance of the first impression, and the refinement of social skills, businesses are returning to the winning formula of success—striving to be the best for the customer, knowing that the bottom line will take care of itself if the needs of the customer come first. The Business of Manners Seminar provides intensive corporate training that's designed to empower your team with the skills needed to ensure personal success and the success of the company.

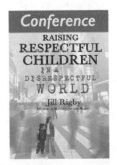

Raising Respectful Children in a Disrespectful World Conference

Don't stop with the reading of this book . . . there's more, much more. Bring the Raising Respectful Children in a Disrespectful World parenting conference to your community. Jill Rigby will personally host your event and present her timeless truths and insights along with other parenting experts. This powerful, home-changing experience will make a difference in your community.

For booking:
Manners of the Heart Community Fund
225 767.3696[p]   225 767.3695[f]
www.thecommunityofmanners.com

♥ Notes ♥

♥ Notes ♥

♥ Notes ♥

♥ Notes ♥

♥ Notes ♥

♥ Notes ♥

♥ Notes ♥